Building Alliances

A How-To Manual to Support Transitioning Youth

Valerie L. Mazzotti
Dawn A. Rowe

Council for Exceptional Children

Division on Career Development and Transition

Council for Exceptional Children
3100 Clarendon Blvd., Suite 600
Arlington, VA 22201
www.cec.sped.org

Library of Congress Cataloging-in-Publication data

Mazzotti, Valerie L.
Building alliances: A how-to manual to support transitioning youth / by Valerie L. Mazzotti and Dawn A. Rowe.
p. cm.
Includes biographical references.

ISBN 978-0-86586-495-5 (soft cover)
ISBN 978-0-86586-496-2 (eBook)
CEC Product Number P6145

Cover by Devall Design.
Design by Tom Karabatakis.

Printed in the United States of America by Gasch Printing.

First edition

10 9 8 7 6 5 4 3

Contents

Introduction
Collaborating to Deliver Effective Transition Services

Over the last two decades, postschool outcomes for youth with disabilities have improved, but these youth are not experiencing postschool outcomes at the same rate as their typically developing peers in the areas of education, employment, and independent living (Newman et al., 2011). Research indicates that when youth with disabilities access collaborative services during high school, they are more likely to experience positive postschool outcomes (Noonan, Gaumer-Erikson, & Morningstar, 2013; Test et al., 2009). To ensure these youth have the skills and supports needed for a successful postschool life, school personnel and community service providers should collaborate throughout the transition planning process to support youth with disabilities in all aspects of the school environment while they are still in high school. According to the Individuals With Disabilities Education Act (IDEA, 2006), *transition* is

> A coordinated set of activities for a student with a disability that is designed to be within a results oriented process, that is focused on improving the academic and functional achievement of the child with a disability to facilitate the child's movement from school to post-school activities, including postsecondary education, vocational education, integrated employment (including supported employment), continuing and adult education, adult services, independent living, or community participation. (34 C.F.R. § 300.43[a][1])

Defining transition services as a "coordinated set of activities" makes collaboration among stakeholders at the secondary and postsecondary levels a key factor in implementing the law. Therefore, *effective collaboration*, defined as an "interactive process characterized by mutual respect, trust, and open communication" (Campbell-Whatley & Lyons, 2013, p. 129), is necessary to support students' transition into postschool life.

Successful transition planning requires a partnership among students, families, school-age service or program providers, postschool service or program providers, and local community members to ensure the process supports youth with disabilities (Benz, Lindstrom, & Halpern, 1995; Hands, 2010; Kohler & Field, 2003). A collaborative transition team should meet regularly to plan and coordinate services to ensure youth with disabilities have a satisfactory transition experience that provides opportunities for meaningful work and living environments postschool (Test, Aspel, & Everson, 2006). These kinds of collaborative partnerships predict positive postschool outcomes for youth with disabilities (Rowe et al., 2015; Test et al., 2009). For example, Bullis, Davis, Bull, and Johnson (1995) found that students with disabilities who received support from three or more agencies in high school were more than twice as likely to engage in employment and educational opportunities postschool than students who received support from two or fewer agencies. In addition, Repetto, Webb, Garvan, and Washington (2002) found that interagency council activities, such as creating agency directories, providing general information to stakeholders, and forming local business advisory boards is positively correlated with postschool success for students with disabilities. Last, several qualitative studies have found that collaborative efforts among educational, community, and adult service agencies appear to generate more positive postschool outcomes for individuals with disabilities (Collet-Klingenberg, 1998; Devlieger & Trach, 1999; Gowdy, Carlson, & Rapp, 2003).

Further, Test et al. (2009) conducted a systematic review of secondary transition correlational literature and found interagency collaboration to be an in-school predictor of positive postschool outcomes in the areas of education and employment for students with disabilities. Although administrators and scholars agree collaboration is an important practice that positively correlates with improved postschool outcomes, a lack of collaboration continues to exist among families, schools, communities, and adult service providers (Benz, Lindstrom, & Latta, 1999; Johnson, Bruininks, & Thurlow, 1987; Katsiyannis, Zhang, Woodruf, & Dixon, 2005). This lack of coordination poses difficulties for students with disabilities as they transition from high school to adult life.

There are two types of collaborative partnerships that must be in place to effectively support youth with disabilities during and after high school: intra-agency collaboration and interagency collaboration. *Intra-agency* is collaboration within the school district (Test et al., 2006). Interagency collaboration is a partnership between two or more organizations to share resources (Test et al., 2006). Each of these types of collaborative partnerships has specific team members and requirements (see Table I.1). In this book, our discussions regarding collaboration include both intra-agency and interagency collaboration, with distinctions made for specific partners.

Collaboration requires communication across agencies, programs, and other entities. To facilitate a successful transition into postschool life for youth with disabilities, collaboration should work as "a clear, purposeful, and carefully designed process" (Rowe et al., 2015, p. 122). Effective collaboration requires developing a common vision and mission; sharing resources; and implementing policies, practices, and procedures that support students with disabilities and their families at the level required by individual transition needs. This kind of collaboration is integral to developing a network of people who can provide services and resources for students who need transition-related support (Noonan, 2014; Rowe et al., 2015).

Collaboration—In Practice

To facilitate collaboration between schools and community service providers, schools must implement coordinated transition programs that include effective collaboration practices. Researchers have attempted to develop strategies and models to study the effects of collaboration on transition outcomes for youth with disabilities, and several models have been developed to support a collaborative transition process (see Table I.2).

Recently, the Council for Exceptional Children's Division for Career Development and Transition (CEC-DCDT) revised the professional standards and ethics for the field of special education in transition (CEC, 2013). The new transition standards were developed to ensure that professionals are well prepared to support the individualized transition needs of youth with disabilities. The standards include seven areas of competency:

1. Use valid and reliable assessments.
2. Use knowledge of general and specialized curricula to improve programs, supports, and services at classroom, school, community, and system levels.
3. Facilitate the continuous improvement of general and special education programs, supports, and services at the classroom, school, and system levels for individuals with exceptionalities.
4. Conduct, evaluate, and use inquiry to guide professional practice.
5. Provide leadership to formulate goals, set and meet high professional expectations, advocate for effective policies and evidence-based practices, and create positive and productive work environments.
6. Use foundational knowledge of the field and professional ethical principles and practice standards to inform special education practice, engage in lifelong learning, advance the profession, and perform leadership responsibilities to promote the success of individuals with exceptionalities and professional colleagues.
7. Collaborate with stakeholders to improve programs, services, and outcomes for individuals with exceptionalities and their families.

Table I.1. Collaborative Partnerships		
Type of partnership	**Team members**	**Responsibilities**
Intra-agency (within the school district)	• School personnel • Related service providers • General and special education teachers • Students with disabilities • Families	• Defining schoolwide vision • Effective communication • Clarifying stakeholder roles • Appropriate case management of students • Establishment of procedures for evaluation and for determining outcomes • Follow-up to ensure the needs of youth with disabilities are met
Interagency (between two or more organizations)	• Students or youth with disabilities • Families • School personnel • Community service providers[a] • Employers	• Bridging the gap between services provided to student while in school and postschool • Facilitating joint planning among members • Increasing families' and students' comfort level with the transition process • Ensuring youth begin adult life on a productive path.

Note. See Noonan, 2014, and Test et al., 2006.
[a] May include vocational rehabilitation providers, independent living centers, postsecondary education institutes.

Table I.2. Collaborative Transition Models		
Model	**Type/ Characteristics**	**Features**
Youth Transition Program (YTP; Benz et al., 1999)	School-to-work transition model; multilevel system of collaboration	YTP necessitates collaboration between local school districts, universities, and vocational rehabilitation providers and has been a model for supporting youth with disabilities in transition for over 20 years. The YTP model includes • transition planning, • educational support and instruction, • services for employment, • one-on-one individualized support, and • placement in postsecondary competitive employment and enrollment in postsecondary education or training courses.
Project SEARCH (Rutkowski, Daston, VanKuiken, & Riehle, 2006)	School-to-work collaborative interagency model; designed to support youth with severe disabilities	Partnerships among schools, employers, and vocational rehabilitation providers to facilitate school-to-work transition; employment skill development; and other support to youth with severe intellectual disabilities, autism, and physical disabilities.
Individualized Career Planning (Condon & Callahan, 2008)	School-to-work collaborative model	Includes a collaborative process for conducting transition assessment, developing an employment profile, and identifying methods for facilitating customized employment for students with disabilities.
Communicating Interagency Relationships and Collaborative Linkages for Exceptional Students (CIRCLES; Aspel, Bettis, Quinn, Test, & Wood, 1999; Povenmire-Kirk, Crump, Dieglemann, & Schnorr, 2013)	Multilevel interagency collaborative model	Identifies community-, school-, and individual-level teams, each of which has a specific purpose. Provides opportunities for transition partners: • school personnel communicate on a regular basis about transition-related issues, • community service providers take an active role in the transition planning process, and • school personnel and community service providers communicate on a regular basis.

Standard 7 also specifies three key areas of knowledge and skills required for special education personnel to facilitate effective collaborative practices: (a) using culturally responsive practices to enhance collaboration; (b) using collaborative skills to improve programs, services, and outcomes; and (c) collaborating to promote understanding, resolve conflicts, and build consensus. The standards include three knowledge competencies and 11 skill competencies (see Table I.3) for transition personnel, which we address in this book. Chapter 1 outlines the **roles and responsibilities** of educators, employers, and other stakeholders; Chapter 2 provides some **recommended strategies for collaborating** with stakeholders; Chapter 3 presents methods for **disseminating transition information and resources** to stakeholders; and Chapter 4 proposes ways to **coordinate interagency agreements**. Each chapter includes examples of how to apply the collaboration knowledge and skills competencies.

Table I.3. CEC–DCDT Collaboration Competencies for Transition Personnel	
Knowledge	**Skills**
• Roles and responsibilities of educators, employers, and other stakeholders in a variety of settings related to postsecondary outcomes. • Employment trends and needs in the community. • Strategies for collaborating with stakeholders to ensure and increase effective transition services, supports, and outcomes for youth with disabilities and their families.	• Promote active involvement of families, especially those from culturally and linguistically diverse backgrounds, throughout the transition decision-making and implementation processes. • Coordinate interagency agreements and partnerships to use and share data to achieve postsecondary outcomes. • Communicate with employers and other professionals to develop and monitor natural support networks. • Disseminate transition information and resources to stakeholders. • Participate in community-level transition teams. • Ensure compliance with federal and state policies impacting transition (e.g., Fair Labor Standards Act). • Implement student and family referrals to postsecondary and community services. • Coordinate work-based programs (e.g., work-study or paid work). • Communicate regularly with employers, businesses, and worksite personnel. • Plan accommodations and modifications in postsecondary, educational, and training settings. • Develop job placements within the community and coordinate placement activities with relevant agencies.

Note. Adapted with permission from *Specialty Set: CEC Advanced Special Education Transition Specialist.* Copyright 2013 by the Council for Exceptional Children.

Researchers have attempted to develop strategies and models to study the effects of collaboration on transition outcomes for youth with disabilities, and several models have been developed to support a collaborative transition process.

Collaboration in Multitiered Frameworks

Given the recognized importance of collaboration in the transition planning process, it is important to identify sustainable models of collaboration that fit within existing high school frameworks. Many schools have adopted a multitiered system of support (MTSS) to address both academic and behavioral needs in ways that will prepare students for postschool life (see Figure I.1). An MTSS requires collaboration among multiple systems (e.g., general and special education personnel, families, community partners) in order to engage in data-based decision making and implement appropriate evidence-based interventions to meet the needs of all students. Further, an MTSS can provide a systematic approach to ensure student success in secondary school (Thomas & Dykes, 2011).

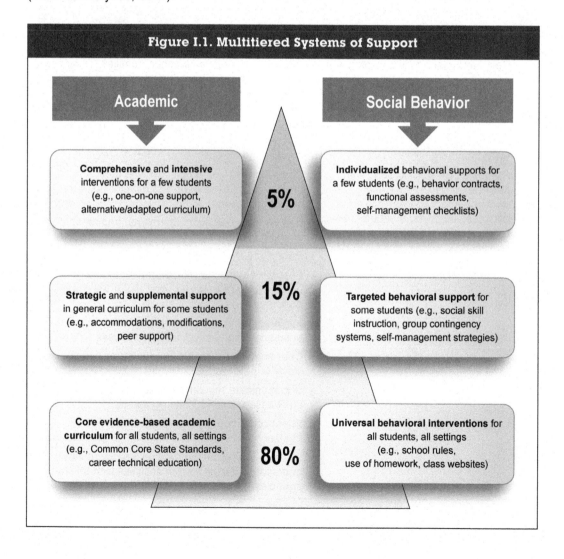

Figure I.1. Multitiered Systems of Support

In 2010, the U.S. Department of Education funded a collaborative effort by the National High School Center, the National Center on Response to Intervention, and the Center on Instruction to create the High School Tiered Interventions Initiative. This initiative was established to increase understanding of how tiered intervention models can be used in high schools across the country (National High School Center, National Center on Response to Intervention, & Center on Instruction, 2010). Several contextual factors that support tiered interventions as effective at the high school level have been identified, including student and family involvement and stakeholder engagement. These entities must collaborate to identify evidence-based instructional strategies and assessment tools required to support the secondary transition needs of students with disabilities (National High School Center et al., 2010).

Collaboration is a necessary part of the process for all students and a key component to effective implementation of multitiered frameworks (Hein, Smerdon, & Sambolt, 2013). Considering an MTSS at the secondary level includes providing supports across a continuum of services with varying degrees of collaborative partnership. These partnerships provide a variety of experiences and knowledge to support the vision and mission of the group (Hentz & Jones, 2011).

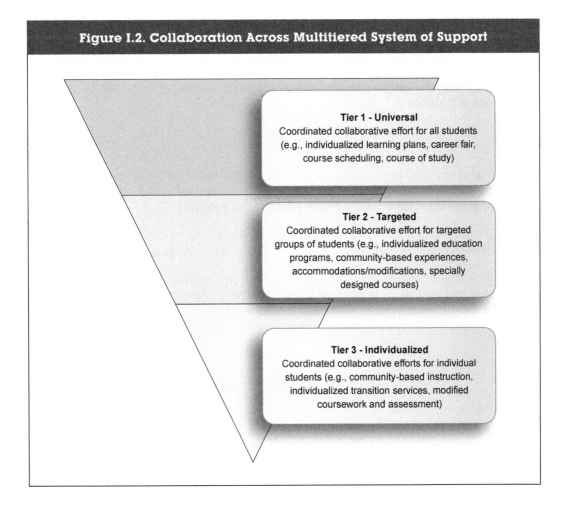

Figure I.2. Collaboration Across Multitiered System of Support

Tier 1 - Universal
Coordinated collaborative effort for all students (e.g., individualized learning plans, career fair, course scheduling, course of study)

Tier 2 - Targeted
Coordinated collaborative effort for targeted groups of students (e.g., individualized education programs, community-based experiences, accommodations/modifications, specially designed courses)

Tier 3 - Individualized
Coordinated collaborative efforts for individual students (e.g., community-based instruction, individualized transition services, modified coursework and assessment)

At the secondary level, transition fits within an MTSS and supports all students with disabilities, regardless of disability type (Morningstar, Bassett, Kochhar-Bryant, Cashman, & Wehmeyer, 2012; Morningstar, Gaumer-Erikson, & Noonan, 2009; Thomas & Dykes, 2011). Morningstar and Clark (2003) developed a multitiered framework for transition, which includes a tiered model for collaboration among students, families, schools, and communities (see Figure I.2). At Tier 1 of an MTSS, coordinated collaborative efforts involve all students. This may include efforts to develop school and district improvement plans, school–business partnerships, schoolwide assessment protocols, career fairs, and individualized learning plans to support the transition needs of all students (Test, Morningstar, Lombardi, & Fowler, 2013). At Tier 1, collaboration may also occur in efforts to identify appropriate courses of study and to schedule coursework. At Tier 2, coordinated collaborative efforts target groups of students. For example, some students require more support for transition both in school and in the community (Test et al., 2013). At Tier 2, key stakeholders may collaborate to design and develop individualized education programs (IEPs) and community-based experiences (e.g., visiting disability services at the local college or job shadowing). At this tier, collaborators may also identify accommodations and modifications to support student success in the general curriculum or in specially designed courses (e.g., career technical education) to support students' career interests. Finally, at Tier 3, coordinated collaborative efforts focus on individual students. For example, key stakeholders may develop individualized community-based instructional experiences or transition services (Test et al., 2013). At this tier, students may also receive modified coursework and assessments necessary to support their individual needs. We discuss strategies for providing collaborative transition services across tiers in Chapter 1.

Summary

 Successful transition planning requires collaborative partnerships among stakeholders who, when working together, can build the momentum needed to improve outcomes for youth with disabilities.

 The development of such collaboration should focus on methods and models that fit within the existing context of the school (e.g., MTSS).

 To facilitate collaborative partnerships, it is also important that schools build staff capacity (e.g., special education teachers and transition specialists) to carry out the roles and responsibilities defined by the CEC-DCDT collaboration knowledge and skills competencies.

Chapter 1

Find the Right People: Identifying Critical Stakeholders

CEC-DCDT Collaboration Competencies for Transition Personnel addressed in this chapter...

Knowledge	Skills
• Roles and responsibilities of educators, employers, and other stakeholders in a variety of settings related to postsecondary outcomes.	• Promote active involvement of families, especially those from culturally and linguistically diverse communities, throughout the transition decision-making and implementation processes. • Communicate with employers and other professionals to develop and monitor natural support networks. • Disseminate transition information and resources to stakeholders. • Participate in community-level transition teams.

For students to successfully transition to postschool activities, stakeholders must collaborate. *Stakeholders* include, but are not limited to, students with disabilities, families, school personnel, employers, and community service providers. During school, youth can be inundated with the programs and services provided by different individuals (e.g., general education teachers, special education teachers, speech and language pathologists, transition specialists, guidance counselors). Although these individuals offer different services, they share the same ultimate goal: to prepare youth for postsecondary education, employment, and independent living (Hein, Smerdon, & Sambolt, 2013). In order to achieve this goal, these individuals must communicate on a regular basis and collaborate with one another to align all services in preparation for a successful transition.

One challenge youth and families face during the postsecondary transition process is the shift from entitlement of services to a system in which youth must meet eligibility requirements (Steere, Rose, & Cavaiuolo, 2007). The Individuals With Disabilities Education Act (IDEA, 2006) requires state education agencies (SEAs) and local education agencies (LEAs) to provide students with disabilities a free, appropriate public education. Therefore, the K–12 educational system is a system of *entitlement*. Special education and related services are required to meet an individual's unique needs and to provide preparation for further education, employment, and independent living (Wood, Kelley, Test, & Fowler, 2010).

Adult service agencies operate to the contrary. The community service system is one of *eligibility*: Individuals must meet the particular requirements of each agency in order to receive services (Wood et al., 2010). Many individuals with disabilities fail to access services after high school due to a lack of knowledge about different agencies, the services provided, and the requirements and processes for accessing them. It is because of the differences in service delivery between school and community agencies that school and agency personnel must work together to assist students with disabilities as they transition from secondary school to the adult world. Students, especially, can be daunted by the task of proving themselves eligible for services; this process will be much less frustrating if youth, families, schools, and community service providers collaborate to make the transition seamless (Steere et al., 2007).

There are several types of collaborative partnerships that can occur for the purposes of transition planning (Noonan, 2014); all transition partnerships, however, fall under three main categories of teams. **Community-level teams** connect schools, a district, or multiple districts with the community. **School-level teams** support the transition planning efforts for all youth in the school, and **individual-level teams** support the transition needs of individual students. Table 1.1 describes the purpose, participants, and activities of each of these teams.

Table 1.1. Collaborative Transition Teams	
Community-level team	
Purpose	**Participants**
The team's overarching purpose is to improve postsecondary outcomes for youth with disabilities in the community. The composition of the team enables schools and communities to build a sustainable system of service delivery by aligning secondary transition programs, practices, and services with community service systems.	Director of special education School principal Transition specialist School board member Employer Postsecondary education representative (e.g., someone from the community college or university) Family members Community service agencies/provider (e.g., vocational rehabilitation providers, workforce development organizations, local transportation providers, Chambers of Commerce, group homes, advocacy groups)
Activities	
The community-level team provides administrative leadership for a range of postsecondary transition services. The team makes and modifies policy; members work together to identify solutions to problems or overcome barriers within local schools and the community. Community-level teams generally meet about two to four times a year. Team activities include: • identifying community-based resources; • developing, implementing, and revising interagency agreements; • coordinating activities for staff professional development; • using data-based decision making for program improvement and evaluation; • identifying strategies to improve transition programs, practices, and services; • establishing support networks for families and youth with disabilities; and • sharing information with stakeholders to support youth with disabilities in employment and postsecondary settings.	

Table 1.1. Collaborative Transition Teams (cont'd)

School-level team

Purpose	Participants
The purpose of the team is to ensure continued support for its students with disabilities; its efforts provide a framework within which to support individual students in the school.	Student Family member(s) Transition specialist Special education teacher Career or technical education teacher General education teacher Case managers from community service agencies

Activities

The school-level team works directly with families and students to facilitate a transition planning process based around a "student-centered planning philosophy" (Aspel et al., 1999, p. 7). They typically meet monthly to share information and conduct preplanning activities to support individual-level teams in developing transition IEPs. School-level team responsibilities include:

- developing timelines for the delivery of community services;
- identifying areas of need in transition service delivery and designating appropriate team members to address those areas;
- assisting students and families in identifying barriers and solutions to service delivery;
- evaluating transition programs, practices, and services and recommending changes as needed for individual students; and
- developing a system to transfer case management from the school to community service agencies.

Individual-level team

Purpose	Participants
The purpose of the team is to develop an effective transition plan for the individual student.	Student Family member(s) Transition specialist Special education teacher General education teacher LEA representative Related service provider Community service provider

Activities

Individual-level team meetings can occur at any time during the school year and should be convened when needed to develop or revise a student's transition plan. Team responsibilities include:

- using assessment data, including input from students and families, to develop measurable postschool IEP goals in the areas of education, employment, and independent living;
- identifying transition services that will reasonably enable the student to meet the postschool goals;
- ensuring the student's course of study will reasonably enable the student to meet the postschool goals;
- ensuring that annual IEP goals will reasonably enable the student to reach his or her postschool goals; and
- ensuring the student, family members, and community service representatives are invited to IEP meetings and have the opportunity to contribute to the decision-making process.

Note. Some members of teams may "cross over" to a different team; for example, a school-level team member might also serve on the community-level team. Support for individual students—at both the school level and individual level—is based on individual student needs; for example, students with severe disabilities may require more support from multiple community service agencies (e.g., vocational rehabilitation, mental health, independent living centers) than others (e.g., student with mild learning disability requiring disability services at local community college). For additional information on the different types of collaborative transition teams and their activities, see Aspel, Bettis, Quinn, Test, & Wood, 1999; Fixsen, Blasé, Duda, Naoom, & VanDyke, 2009; Noonan, 2014; Povenmire-Kirk, Crump, Dieglemann, & Schnorr, 2013; and Test, Aspel, & Everson, 2006. IEP = individualized education program; LEA = local education agency.

Research in Practice

The Caper School District is a midsized urban school district located in the Northwest United States. The school district serves eight high schools and includes a diverse student population. Students with mild to severe disabilities receive services until the age of 21. Understanding the need for effective collaboration to ensure all students with disabilities in the district experience both positive in-school and postschool outcomes, the Special Education Director, Sophia Alverez, has investigated a variety of collaboration models. She has decided to implement the Communicating Interagency Relationships and Collaborative Linkages for Exceptional Students (CIRCLES) model. Using CIRCLES, Sophia will adapt a team approach to transition planning for students with disabilities and her first step will be to identify the critical players in the transition planning process from the school district and the Caper community, including students, families, school- and district-level personnel (e.g., general education, related services, career technical education teachers, business leaders, adult service providers, and postsecondary education partners).

Stakeholder Roles and Responsibilities

Each key stakeholder on a transition team, regardless of the team level, has a specific role and responsibility in the collaborative transition planning process (see Table 1.2).

Students With Disabilities

A student with a disability should be recognized as the leader in the transition planning process and should participate by attending and actively participating in transition planning meetings and other transition activities. Students need to take ownership of their education and capitalize on the continuum of services and supports available. By participating, they not only provide information about strengths, needs, and preferences, but also provide guidance related to skill development and abilities—essential to pursuing postsecondary goals (Hughes & Carter, 2012).

Students can contribute to transition planning in a variety of valuable ways. They should be encouraged to demonstrate a positive attitude, a willingness to learn at school and in the community, and a readiness to develop the skills needed to achieve their goals.

Families

Along with youth with disabilities, families (i.e., parents, guardians, extended family members) are the most important stakeholders in the transition planning process—and can provide critical information to help identify a student's interests, strengths, needs, and abilities. Families also foster independence by supporting the student and the school system in the student's transition to postsecondary education, employment, and independent living.

No later than middle school, families should help their children identify what the postsecondary future looks like (i.e., college, career) and what supports will be needed to be successful. These early decisions can have long-term consequences that affect the rest of the student's life. For example, choosing not to seek information or apply for assistance from a community service agency in a timely way may result in a young adult living in a community without needed supports, in turn causing unnecessary financial and emotional strain (for both the youth and the family). Similarly young adults who are not prepared to advocate for themselves on the job may jeopardize their employment prospects; others may end up struggling unnecessarily in a post-secondary education environment instead of receiving academic accommodations. Simply put, students and families must contribute in decision making at all stages of transition planning. This includes attending meetings; assisting in writing the IEP; and taking advantage of the multitude of opportunities for instruction, assessment, and services provided during high school.

Special Education Teachers

Special education teachers participate in both the school-level and individual-level teams, acting as primary coordinators of transition services for youth with disabilities (Flexer, Baer, Luft, & Simmons, 2013) and lead the individual-level team in developing the transition plan (Aspel et al., 1999; Povenmire-Kirk et al., 2013). In this role, special education teachers:

- Ensure students and families participate in the transition planning process.
- Review all information related to the student's academic and functional performance levels and future goals.
- Develop the transition components of the IEP.
- Provide additional information about the transition planning process.
- Address any other relevant student issues.

General Education Teachers

The term *general education teacher* refers to teachers who provide academic instruction to youth in the general curriculum as well as teachers who provide career-focused instruction (e.g., career technical education) to youth. The general education teacher is a required member of the transition planning team and contributes knowledge about how to access the general curriculum and how to acquire the skills needed for post-secondary education and employment settings.

Related Service Providers

Related service providers assume many roles and may include speech and language pathologists, audiologists, interpreters, psychologists, social workers, school nurses, physical and occupational therapists, recreation therapists, counselors (including rehabilitation counseling), and orientation and mobility specialists. Additional related service providers may be identified based on the individual needs of a student. These individuals support general and special educators in delivering instructional content that will improve both academic and functional skills while providing necessary related services to students. Related service providers assist the IEP team in determining appropriate postsecondary supports (e.g., assistive technology or job coaching) and may initiate conversations with postsecondary service providers on behalf of the student and the family.

Transition Specialists

Transition specialists, also called *transition coordinators*, should be included in the collaboration process; Noonan, Morningstar, and Gaumer-Erickson (2008) recommend all secondary special education programs include a transition specialist to help facilitate the collaborative process. However, not all SEAs and LEAs fund transition specialists for special education support at the school or district levels; therefore, many special education teachers will assume this role.

Transition specialists can play an important role in ensuring (a) career and vocational programs exist to support student skill development, (b) community service providers participate in the transition planning process, and (c) relevant teams work together to develop and identify community resources to support youth with disabilities both in-school and postschool (Blalock et al., 2003).

School District Personnel

Both school and district personnel are key stakeholders in the collaboration process and can provide valuable insight and support to youth with disabilities as they move through the transition process. As a member of a community-level team, school and district administrators support both general and special education teachers in the collaborative process. Administrators facilitate transition services delivery by participating on community-level teams charged with providing leadership for the array of transition services offered. They also assist in finding solutions for problems that may arise during service delivery (Aspel et al., 1999)

As members of school-level and individual-level transition planning administrators help ensure the educational services specified in individual students' transition plans are being delivered. At a minimum, they provide teachers with access to curricula for teaching transition-related skills that will support the student's progress towards achieving postschool goals and support teachers in decision making and planning.

Community Service Providers

Transition planning is a complex process involving many school personnel, students, and families. School and district personnel cannot transition students from school to postsecondary life alone; for a smooth transition and to improve postschool outcomes, they must collaborate with community service providers. Organizations outside the K-12 system can collaborate with schools to improve postschool outcomes. These organizations include but are not limited to adult service providers (e.g., vocational rehabilitation [VR] providers, local departments of mental health or developmental disabilities), postsecondary education institutions, the United States Social Security Administration [SSA], One-Stop Career Centers, independent living centers, and local business and industry.

Key community players in transition include (see Steere, Rose, & Cavaiuolo, 2007):

- **VR**: Assists persons with cognitive, sensory, physical, or emotional disabilities to attain employment and increased independence. VR may provide apprenticeship programs, vocational training, and college training towards a vocational goal.
- **SSA**: Provides benefits to people of any age who are unable to do substantial work and have severe physical or mental disabilities. Programs offered through the SSA include Social Security Disability Insurance, Supplemental Security

Income, Plans to Achieve Self-Support, Medicaid, and Medicare. Work incentive programs may include cash benefits and insurance while working; help with extra work expenses because of a disability, and assistance to start a new line of work. Financial incentives for further education and training are also available.

- **Mental health and developmental disability services**: Provide a comprehensive system of services responsive to the needs of individuals with mental illness or developmental disabilities. Services through such agencies could include supported employment, competitive employment support, case management services, therapeutic recreation, respite, and residential services.

- **Postsecondary education institutions (universities, community colleges, and technical schools):** Universities offer bachelor's degrees and higher in a variety of fields of study. Community colleges offer an array of certificate and associate's degree programs for students. Technical schools provide students with relevant and technological skills needed to meet the demands of current industries.

- **Goodwill Industries:** Provides education, training, and career services for people with disadvantages such as welfare dependency, homelessness, and lack of education or work experience, as well as those with physical, mental, and emotional disabilities. Goodwill professionals provide services such as helping locate childcare support and transportation, counseling, and life-skills programs.

- **One-Stop Career Centers:** Provide a variety of services to help employers and jobseekers meet their work development needs. Most services offered through One Stop are free. Staff is available to help individuals with job searching and placement, resume writing, job service registration, unemployment insurance claim filing. One Stop also furnishes information on other community resources and programs. There are a range of different assessments available through the One Stop center as well as career counseling, job skills classes, and assistance in developing an individual employment plan. Also available are levels of job training.

- **Independent living centers (ILCs):** Provide services to maximize the independence of individuals with disabilities and the accessibility of their communities. Core services include advocacy, independent living skills training, information and referral, and peer counseling. Other services may be provided depending on local context.

Community partners and organizations also collaborate with schools and districts on community involvement opportunities for students. They may consult with other adult service providers and schools to identify level of support needed based on each student's strengths and needs. In addition, they may consult with local businesses to provide information regarding skills and abilities needed for success in those workplaces (Steere et al., 2007). Figure 1.1 is a letter template that special education teachers can use to invite community service agency representatives to participate in individual-level team meetings. When complete, sign the letter and make a copy for your records. To locate community service providers in your area, refer to the discussion in Chapter 3 on community mapping.

	Participates in...			
Team member	Individual-level team	School-level team	Community-level team	Responsibilities and activities
Table 1.2. Transition Team Members				
Students	✓	✓		Advocate for themselves and provide input about their transition planning needs. Student participation in transition planning should include: • communicating interests, strengths, needs, preferences, and postsecondary goals through formal or informal assessments, pre-transition planning discussions, instructional lessons, and so on; • identifying other people they want involved in their transition planning process (e.g., family, friends, mentor) who can form a support network to help facilitate the student's transition to postschool life.
Family members	✓	✓	✓	Assist the student in making decisions about education and transition plans. Role will differ depending on the cultural context and individual circumstances; however, families should be involved in • pre-transition planning activities, • transition planning meetings, • student assessment, • service delivery, • evaluation of the student's transition program, and • identifying and establishing the natural supports (e.g., a network, mentors, trainers) individual students need to be successful after high school. Families also can assist with generalizing the skills learned in school to the home and community setting.
Special education teachers	✓	✓		Serve as liaison between families, students, teachers, employers, community service agencies, and community resources. They support youth and families throughout the transition process. Special education teachers' responsibilities may include: • working with general educators to embed transition-related instruction and identify appropriate accommodations and modifications for individual students, • facilitate collaboration among stakeholders, • identify and coordinate pre-transition planning activities (e.g., family and friend support networks), and • provide direct instruction of transition-related skills to students in both the classroom and the community.
General education teachers	✓	✓		In addition to providing direct instruction, collaborate with special education teachers and other stakeholders on curriculum, accommodations, and modifications to promote student involvement in general education coursework. General education teachers are responsible for: • monitoring and communicating student progress to other members of the student's IEP team; • providing accommodations and modifications as delineated by students' education plans, and ensuring these are incorporated into state-mandated testing; and • supporting students' transition goals as these relate to the general curriculum.

Team member	Participates in...			Responsibilities and activities
	Individual-level team	School-level team	Community-level team	
Related service providers	✓	✓		Individual specialists, selected on the basis of a student's particular needs or challenges, collaborate with special education teachers, families, and other stakeholders to support youth with disabilities. Related service providers: • assist in development and implementation of transition plans, including identifying appropriate postsecondary supports; • provide documentation to the team regarding the nature, frequency, and amount of related services to be provided; and • document and report on student progress.
Transition specialists	✓	✓	✓	Ensure that students with disabilities receive transition services in accordance with federal guidelines. Their role is to provide overall coordination of transition services, to ensure individual students' needs are being met. Transition specialists may: • act as an intermediary for schools, districts, and community supports; • provide professional development and training to district personnel; and • oversee or participate in districtwide transition programming.
School district personnel	✓	✓	✓	Assist the student in identifying postsecondary goals in the area of education, employment, training, and independent living. This includes identifying other individuals and community resources that may assist students in developing and achieving these goals, as well as managing the process of supporting students in applying for needed services. The school district/local education agency responsibilities include: • reviewing students' annual progress toward transition goals, • providing students with a Summary of Performance upon exiting, • managing interagency agreements, • coordinating staff development activities, and • overseeing student/family education about the special education and transition process.
Community service providers	✓		✓	Support students as they move from a system of entitlement to a system of eligibility, coordinating postsecondary services. Various community service providers collaborate with school districts on program planning and development for students, including: • coordinating requests for information and consulting with special and general education teachers, including career technical education teachers and vocational educators; • conducting functional vocational assessments, providing on-the-job and vocational training and job placement; • determining eligibility for services (e.g., Social Security, Medicaid); • providing assistive technology and health services; • leisure opportunities; and • arranging funding for postsecondary educational opportunities.

Note. For additional information on team member roles and responsibilities, see Flexer et al., 2013; Hughes & Carter, 2012; and Rowe et al., 2015. IEP = individualized education program.

Figure 1.1. Letter to Community Service Providers

Insert name of the school
Insert school street address (city, state zip code)
Insert date (month, day, year)
Insert name of adult agency representative
Insert name of agency
Insert agency address

RE: Insert first and last name of student

Dear Insert name of agency representative,

During Insert student's name Individualized Education Program (IEP) meeting this year, we will discuss long term planning. We will look at where Insert student's name is going when completing school, what skills need to be developed in order to get there, and what linkages to other agencies may be necessary. The goal is to work together to ensure that Insert student's name has the opportunity to become employable by developing the academic, social, and living skills needed to make the transition from school to work (or further education) and community living. We would like to invite you to participate in this meeting and share the available services and supports offered by your agency. We would also be interested in hearing about your organization's eligibility criteria.

The meeting details are as follows:
Insert meeting date and time
Insert meeting location
Insert contact information

If you are unable to attend, would you be willing to send the IEP team information regarding services and supports and contact information so that Insert student's name and Insert pronoun: his or her family can contact you at a later date?

We feel that by teaching the skills needed to live, learn, and work in the community, and by providing Insert Student's Name with additional information about adult services and programs, we can better meet the goal for which we are all striving: the successful participation of Insert student's name in adult life.

We look forward to working together toward this goal at the IEP meeting.

Sincerely,

SIGN HERE

Print name

CC: Insert name of IEP case manager, School IEP Case Manager

Research in Practice

In identifying the critical players in the transition planning process for her school district, Sophia identified VR as a key stakeholder and so worked with the VR counselor, Liam Stetson, to determine his role. They agreed he would assist with vocational interest and exploration assessments, work with individual students to develop postschool employment goals, and provide community experiences for students related to employment. In addition, Sophia worked with the general education teacher, Ava Sumner. Together, they determined Ava would identify and administer appropriate academic assessments for students, assist individual students in developing postsecondary goals, and design instruction to assist students in reaching their annual IEP goals.

Collaborative roles and responsibilities of all team members may vary based on students' identified support needs (Storm, O'Leary, & Williams, 2000; Test et al., 2006; Wandry & Pleet, 2009). When a student moves into Tier 2 or Tier 3 of a multitiered system of support, services and supports become much more individualized and require collaboration among many stakeholders. Figure 1.2 is a Collaborative Roles and Responsibilities Tool that special education teachers can use when identifying key stakeholders' roles and responsibilities in the transition planning process. This tool includes the major aspects of transition planning (e.g., transition assessment, postschool goals, course of study, transition services) and can be used to identify individuals with expertise or information related to each. For example, when considering transition assessment, the special education teacher may identify a general education teacher who has knowledge of a student's academic performance. When considering transition services, a related service provider may be responsible for identifying appropriate assistive technologies required to support the student through the transition process. For each student or group of students, a teacher can use this tool to identify the key players and define who will provide the instruction or service. It is important to remember that a stakeholder may assume multiple roles, and their role may change over time given the individual student or the local context (Hentz & Jones, 2011).

Figure 1.2. Collaborative Roles and Responsibilities Tool

Role and responsibility	Group member(s)
Transition assessment	
Academic assessment	
Social-behavioral assessment	
Adaptive behavior/independent living	
Self-determination	
Vocational interest and exploration	
Postschool goals	
Employment	
Education	
Independent living	
Course of study	
State alternatives to regular diploma	
Transition services	
Instruction (academic and functional)	
Related service	
Community experience	
Acquisition of daily living skills	
Postschool adult living objectives	
Functional vocational evaluation	
Annual IEP goals to support postschool goals	
Employment	
Education	
Independent living	
Academic	
Social behavior	
Implementation of transition plan	
Preparation for transition planning meeting	
Participation in transition planning meeting	
Facilitation of goal attainment	

Note. IEP = individualized education program.

Summary

 Stakeholders participating in community-, school-, and individual-level transition teams adopt a variety of roles.

 To ensure students with disabilities a smooth transition to their postsecondary lives, first steps should identify the critical stakeholders at each level and define their individual roles for each case.

 It is important to remember that roles and responsibilities may change according to circumstance and context; an individual stakeholder's role may vary from student to student.

Chapter 2

Put It Together: Building Collaborative Teams

CEC-DCDT Collaboration Competencies for Transition Personnel addressed in this chapter...

Knowledge	Skills
• Roles and responsibilities of educators, employers, and other stakeholders in a variety of settings related to postsecondary outcomes.	• Promote active involvement of families, especially those from culturally and linguistically diverse communities, throughout the transition decision-making and implementation processes.
	• Communicate with employers and other professionals to develop and monitor natural support networks.
	• Disseminate transition information and resources to stakeholders.
	• Participate in community-level transition teams.

Several types of collaborative partnerships can occur when planning and implementing a student's transition to postschool. The need to identify roles and responsibilities of key team members is just the first step in the collaborative process. Community-level teams can be formed to help one or multiple districts connect schools with the community. School-level teams can be developed to support the transition planning efforts for all youth in a school, and individual-level teams can be developed to support the transition needs of individual students. After identifying the roles and responsibilities of collaborative team members, the next step is to pinpoint strategies for building and facilitating the collaborative process.

Building Collaborative Teams

To build an effective team, identify initial members, select a team leader, establish rapport among members, and agree upon a common goal (Blalock, 1996; Noonan, 2014). Fabian, Luecking, and Tilson (1994) suggested five fundamental characteristics that must exist to develop an effective team:

- trust,
- goals and objectives that benefit all stakeholders,
- long-term relationships,
- service competence, and
- customer service orientation.

The foundation of an effective team is based on mutual understanding. Goals should be attainable, stakeholders should avoid making promises they cannot keep, and the team's goals should benefit all stakeholders. Long-term relationships should be developed to sustain the program over time and avoid disconnect caused by staff turnover. Knowledge about each agency's needs and services will also facilitate effective team building, and promote resource sharing and collaborative service delivery. Finally, an effective collaborative team will be customer service oriented, with a primary goal of improving student (customer) outcomes (Fabian et al., 1994). See Chapter 3 for a discussion of strategies for obtaining information about partnering agencies and other collaborative partners.

To establish an effective collaborative team, it is important to develop rapport among members, define a set of common goals, and ensure mutual respect. All of these components are necessary to ensure sustainability of the team overtime. Test, Aspel, and Everson (2006) recommended several questions for consideration (see Table 2.1)

Table 2.1. Developing Effective Transition Teams: Questions to Consider	
Is there a need for a team?	Are teams mandated by the district or the school? Could an individual accomplish the goal(s) alone? What factors support the development of a team?
What are the goals of the team?	What are the community's needs? What are the family and student's needs?
What are the roles and responsibilities of team members?	Who are the key stakeholders? What are the roles and responsibilities of each team member? What information and resources are needed from each member?
What is the process for convening the team?	Is there an agenda to accomplish goals? Is there a timeline for completion of goals? Do we have strategies for communication and conflict management? Do we have a system of accountability?

Facilitating Collaborative Teams

Wehman, Moon, Everson, Wood, and Barcus (1988) identified three models of collaboration: information exchange, responsibility transfer, and collaborative exchange.

Information Exchange

Refers to a transfer of records for students receiving school-related services (e.g., assessment data, demographic information, behavioral information) and referral-related services (e.g., medical, educational, psychological, vocational). During information exchange, there is little or no planned communication or coordination.

Responsibility Transfer

Occurs when the transition planning team determines the sequence of services, to ensure there is no overlap. Responsibility transfer also should align services to ensure uninterrupted delivery when a student exits high school.

Collaborative Exchange

Occurs when schools and community service agencies combine resources to facilitate the student's transition to adult life during the last few years of school. An overlap in service provision will occur with all agencies involved in the planning process. Collaborative exchange is the level of teamwork most effective for students with disabilities and is critical to ensuring a seamless transition (Test et al., 2006; Wehman et al., 1988)—but it won't be successful without an effective team. Collaborative exchange includes formal and informal means of communication and requires effort and planning for success.

Components of Effective Teamwork

Noonan, Morningstar, and Clark (2005) suggested that effective teamwork involves **collaboration, communication, service coordination,** and **networking**. Figure 2.1 illustrates these components of effective teamwork.

Collaboration requires independent agencies to function as one entity to solve problems, share information, and merge resources. In functioning as one entity, independent agencies facilitate communication by ensuring information and resources are exchanged effectively. This kind of **cooperation** obliges individuals and agencies to interact on a regular basis to facilitate

- decision making,
- accountability,
- trust,
- jointly scheduled activities, and
- collaborative planning time.

Service coordination helps youth access school and community services by coordinating resources at individual-level transition planning meetings. Last, **networking** helps transition planning teams identify the range of services available in the community so they can make referrals to other agencies. Networking is one of the most powerful ways to sustain a collaborative effort.

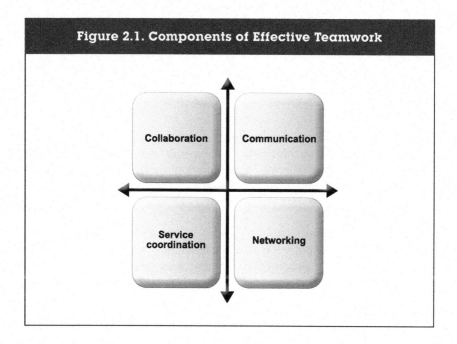

Figure 2.1. Components of Effective Teamwork

Collaboration

Communication

Service coordination

Networking

Four Stages of Collaborative Team Building

When "under construction," collaborative teams typically undergo four stages of development: **forming, storming, norming,** and **performing** (Everson & Guillory, 2002). During the **forming** stage (see Figure 2.2), meeting time focuses on becoming a team and identifying early conceptions of each member's roles and responsibilities. During the **storming** stage, the team works together to develop structural procedures, practice effective communication and conflict management skills, conduct needs assessments, set team goals, and develop action plans.

During the **norming** stage, the team focuses on revising, implementing, and refining team goals and action plans. This stage is outcomes oriented and includes a self-evaluation conducted by the team to assess collaborative efforts. Finally, during the **performing** stage, team members fully collaborate with one another as they develop and implement new and revised action plans. Refer to *The Interagency Teaming Guide* (Everson & Guillory, 2002) for more information on team building and a detailed discussion of the staging process as well as step-by-step instructions for developing collaborative teams.

Working With Collaborative Teams

Collaborative teams can employ a number of strategies to facilitate a smooth transition from high school to postschool life for students with disabilities. In this section, we discuss collaboration strategies for community-level teams as well as for school-level and individual-level teams working within the framework of an existing multitiered system of support (MTSS).

Community-Level Teams

A number of collaborative strategies can be implemented by the community-level team to support youth with disabilities and their families as they move through the transition planning process. Specifically, it is important to consider the capacity of the community to support the transition needs of youth with disabilities and focus on methods for building that capacity (Parent & Wehman, 2011). All members of the community-level team should familiarize themselves with available community service agencies, noting the roles, responsibilities, and services provided by each. This might include visiting local community agencies and meeting with staff members (Parent & Wehman, 2011). Other ways to build capacity involve information sharing. Team members can share information about each agency on school, district, and community service provider websites so families and youth can easily access the information. In addition, the community-level team can distribute flyers with information about the services and supports available through schools and community service providers to local schools, businesses, postsecondary institutions, and recreational and leisure facilities. The team could also develop handbooks for how to access transition services (Hughes & Carter, 2012).

In addition to information sharing, the community-level team can build capacity by working directly with local employers to identify job-related opportunities and worksites that may be appropriate for students at various ability levels. By identifying these opportunities, the community-level team will have a number of options to support youth and place them in work settings that align with the student's preferences, interests, and strengths. Employers can also provide information about the skills and abilities needed for youth with disabilities to be successful in particular employment settings (Steere, Rose, & Cavaiuolo, 2007).

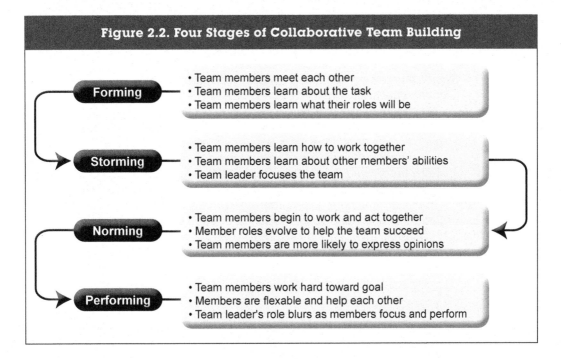

Figure 2.2. Four Stages of Collaborative Team Building

Forming
- Team members meet each other
- Team members learn about the task
- Team members learn what their roles will be

Storming
- Team members learn how to work together
- Team members learn about other members' abilities
- Team leader focuses the team

Norming
- Team members begin to work and act together
- Member roles evolve to help the team succeed
- Team members are more likely to express opinions

Performing
- Team members work hard toward goal
- Members are flexable and help each other
- Team leader's role blurs as members focus and perform

School-Level Teams

For the school-level team, it is important to consider strategies for collaboration within the MTSS (outlined in the Introduction):

- Tier 1 focuses on universal, coordinated collaborative efforts that involve all students.
- Tier 2 focuses on coordinated, collaborative efforts for targeted groups of students.
- Tier 3 focuses on coordinated, collaborative efforts for individual students.

As a student moves into Tier 2 or Tier 3, services and supports become much more individualized and require collaboration among many stakeholders. One primary responsibility of the school-level team should be to identify the critical stakeholders responsible for providing transition activities and services and conducting assessments for youth with disabilities based on individual needs in an MTSS. For example, when considering tiered support, most youth with disabilities will only require the universal support offered at Tier 1. This may include developing their career awareness skills through participation in job shadowing or attending job or college fairs (Test, Morningstar, Lombardi, & Fowler, 2013). However, some youth may require more coordinated collaborative efforts at Tier 2 to support skill development, such as targeted support with opportunities to develop career awareness skills through participating in various job tryouts. *Job tryouts* can help youth identify the occupation that most interests them while helping them pinpoint the skills required for that specific occupation (Test et al., 2013). Further, some youth may require Tier 3 individualized supports, such as participating in on-the-job training with support from a job coach. Table 2.2 illustrates examples of the different services and supports for students within an MTSS.

Research in Practice

Sophia Alverez worked with a school-level team at a high school in Caper to identify critical stakeholders, transition activities, and follow-up assessment for providing collaborative transition services across the tiers. Although the school-level team identified some of the same stakeholders across tiers, they were aware that roles and responsibilities would change based on students' needed supports. Sophia's school-level team used the Collaborative Roles and Responsibilities Tool (see Figure 1.2, Chapter 1) to identify areas of expertise across stakeholders for each area of transition planning. Using the tool to organize this information helped the team understand the roles and responsibilities of each stakeholder. Sophia knew, too, that this tool could be used during preplanning to align students' needs with local community agency services and supports (Parent & Wehman, 2011).

Table 2.2. Providing Collaborative Transition Services Across Tiers

Critical players	Activity	Assessment/Follow-up
Goals related to postsecondary employment		
• Student • Special education teacher • General education teacher	**Tier 1:** Participate in job shadowing	• Informational interview with employer • Career interest inventory
• Student • Special education teacher • Parent • Vocational rehabilitation	**Tier 2:** Attend job try-outs	• Job site analysis • Ecological assessment • Task analysis • Employer interview
• Student • Special education teacher • Parent • Vocational rehabilitation • Other adult service providers	**Tier 3:** Engage in on-the-job training with supports from job coach	• Ecological assessment • Employer evaluation • Functional vocational evaluation
Goals related to postsecondary education		
• Student • Special education teacher • General education teacher • Disability services representative	**Tier 1:** Research community college via website and or printed resources provided by school	• SAT/ACT • Application for admission • Enrollment in community college or university
• Student • Special education teacher • Parent • Disability services representative	**Tier 2:** Visit community college, including disability services	• College placement tests
• Student • Special education teacher • Parent • Vocational rehabilitation • Other adult service providers • Disability services representative	**Tier 3:** Join an 18- to 21-year-old residential program with community college or Think College program Application for admission and enrollment in local community college	• Ecological assessment • Program specific evaluation • Functional vocational evaluation
Goals related to postsecondary independent living		
• Student • Special education teacher • General education teacher	**Tier 1:** Participate in CTE courses such as home consumer science class, parenting, business math	• Performance in CTE • Formative assessment • Completion of CTE coursework
• Student • Special education teacher • Parent • Vocational rehabilitation	**Tier 2:** Simulate instruction in classroom or school related to independent living skills (e.g., using an ATM or grocery shopping)	• Task analysis
• Student • Special education teacher • Parent • Vocational rehabilitation • Other adult service providers	**Tier 3:** Participate in community-based instruction related to independent living skills (e.g., using an ATM or grocery shopping)	• Task analysis • Ecological assessment • Adaptive behavior assessment

Note. CTE = Career Technical Education.

Individual-Level Teams

During individual-level team meetings, the special education teacher and the student facilitate a team conversation around the collaborative transition services that should be included in the student's transition plan. The team should consider the level of support required in addition to the services and supports necessary for the student to attain the identified postschool goals. The individual-level team should communicate with the school-level team regarding needed supports and services based on student abilities across tiers of support; the individual-level team works together to use that information to develop an individualized transition plan for the student.

Barriers to Collaboration

Schools, families, and community service providers may face a number of barriers when providing collaborative services to students with disabilities. Stakeholders should anticipate potential and existing barriers and identify strategies to circumvent any issues that could potentially keep the team from moving forward. Common barriers related to implementation of effective collaboration include lack of family involvement, inadequate interagency agreements, and failure to provide information to the team regarding the roles and responsibilities of each member (Flexer, Baer, Luft, & Simmons, 2013; Johnson, Bruininks, & Thurlow, 1987; Test et al., 2006). Failure to share other kinds of information with stakeholders has also been identified as a barrier. For example, schools may not communicate specific information about the transition planning process with all stakeholders. This information could include the process for participating in transition planning meetings or the student-specific information needed for referral or postschool goals (Flexer et al., 2013; Peterson & Roessler, 1997). Further, barriers may arise regarding the sharing of information among team members, the use of that information, and the need to maintain student information in a confidential manner (Flexer et al., 2013).

Research in Practice

One of the barriers that Sophia and the team identified involved sharing information across agencies related to postschool outcomes for youth with disabilities. Sophia wanted to share postschool outcomes data with the team members to help them determine what was and was not working for students and families, while students are in high school. Sophia was able to share this information because the team anticipated the barrier of sharing private student information across agencies. They therefore developed a memorandum of understanding (MOU) that allowed them to share student data from each of the agencies for the purpose of program improvement (see Chapter 4 for MOU).

Summary

 Providing transition services must be a collaborative process. This includes maintaining up-to-date information regarding student progress, the transition plan, and postschool goals, and sharing that information effectively among team members.

 Good collaborators will also think beyond simple information sharing. They will attend transition planning and referral meetings to develop a coordinated service delivery plan to support students with disabilities in high school in ways that ensure effective services are delivered postschool (Flexer et al., 2013; Mazzotti, 2009).

 Although the community-, school-, and individual-level teams have specific goals, it is imperative that the teams work together and have an open line of communication to (a) anticipate barriers, (b) ensure all needs are met, and (c) sustain efforts over time.

Chapter 3

Put It in Motion: Mapping the Community

CEC-DCDT Collaboration Competencies for Transition Personnel addressed in this chapter...

Knowledge	Skills
• Employment trends and needs in the community.	• Promote active involvement of families, especially those from culturally and linguistically diverse communities, throughout the transition decision-making and implementation processes. • Communicate with employers and other professionals to develop and monitor natural support networks. • Disseminate transition information and resources to stakeholders. • Participate in community-level transition teams. • Implement student and family referrals to postsecondary and community services.

Effective collaboration on behalf of transitioning youth with disabilities cannot happen without involvement from the community. *Collaborative exchange* is the level of collaboration that most involves the community and best serves transitioning students with disabilities (Test, Aspel, & Everson, 2006; Wehman, Moon, Everson, Wood, Barcus, 1988). It requires being aware of all the services and supports available to students and families in the school and the community and identifying issues within the community that may create barriers for a successful transition (Rutgers Safe and Drug Free Schools Community Project, 2009). *Community mapping* is one way to organize information and give direction to meeting a common goal related to secondary transition program planning, allowing youth with disabilities and their families more flexibility as they move from a system of entitlement to one of eligibility.

The primary purpose of community mapping is to improve the transition from secondary school to postschool for youth with disabilities by identifying areas of need and aligning available services and resources from schools, employers, and community service agencies (Stodden, Brown, Galloway, Mrazek, & Noy, 2004).

Test and colleagues (2006) suggested community needs assessments could identify short- and long-term

- needs of youth with disabilities and their families;
- labor market needs; and
- housing, transportation, and other community opportunities (e.g., recreation, leisure).

Needs assessments do not have to be time consuming or expensive. They may include holding a community meeting at the local school or community service location, sending out surveys via e-mail or cell phone, or identifying existing data that may provide information about transition service delivery and outcomes for youth with disabilities (Noonan, 2014; Test et al., 2006). The alignment of resources and identification of service gaps identified by community mapping enable schools and other service providers to realize the range of services available to youth with disabilities in a community, provide the specific supports needed by each youth, and develop new services and supports targeted to fill existing gaps (Noonan, 2014; Stodden et al., 2004).

The Community Mapping Process

Community mapping is a collaborative exercise to develop a map of the resources available in the community. It provides a structure for key stakeholders to use when transition program planning for youth with disabilities. Community mapping identifies the resources that exist in the school and community (and additional areas for collaboration and coordination), and contributes to a seamless transition to postschool life for students with disabilities. The community mapping process is conducted by a team—**a group** of individuals from schools (e.g., teachers, students, parents) and community service agencies (e.g., vocational rehabilitation providers, employers) who are willing to take ownership of transition planning for youth with disabilities in the community. The process of "mapping" identifies needs and resources, articulates goals for transition planning and service delivery, devises and implements strategies and action steps to achieve the vision, and continually evaluates progress. The community mapping process can be accomplished in five straightforward steps:

1. Form a group of individuals from schools (e.g., teachers, students, families) and community service agencies (e.g., VR providers or employers) that care about transition planning for youth with disabilities in the community.
2. Assess the local community through pre-mapping activities, looking specifically for resources that can help the group address an identified area of need.
3. Plan the approach. Start with the team's vision and goals for transition planning and service delivery. Then devise strategies and action steps to help achieve that vision.
4. Implement the plan using measurable action steps that will have a positive effect on the overall goal of the team.
5. Evaluate progress.

Pre-Mapping Activities

Pre-mapping activities can begin as soon as a team is formed. To start, stakeholders in the transition planning process come together and agree on a purpose for the community map. At this stage, they should establish a vision and set goals (i.e., the *forming* and *storming* stages outlined in Chapter 2). Effective communication will be vital to accomplish these tasks in a way that meets each stakeholder's needs (Crane & Mooney, 2005). Team members will likely have many issues they would like to address; however, in order to set reasonable goals it is important for the team to prioritize issues. First, team members should brainstorm possible issues and challenges and write them on a white board, flip chart, or butcher paper, and then use a worksheet (see Figure 3.1) to prioritize the results.

Figure 3.1. Prioritizing Transition Issues	
Directions: Make a list of all the issues regarding secondary transition. Then, as a group, complete this sheet for each issue you are considering. Use this information to help narrow your focus and develop a targeted action plan.	
Issue	
Prevalence/frequency/incidence	
Population(s) affected	
Seriousness/urgency	
Available data sources	
Possible interventions (consider predictors of postschool success)	
Possible impact	
Current interventions addressing issue	
Consequences if not addressed (community level, school level, individual level)	

Note. See also *Healthy People 2010 Toolkit: A Field Guide to Health Planning,* by the Office of Disease Prevention and Health Promotion, Office of Public Health and Science, U.S. Department of Health and Human Services (2002).

After developing a vision, setting goals, and prioritizing issues, the team should determine a process for gathering data on community resources to support post-secondary transition of youth with disabilities. Establishing a process is essential, as it not only defines the activities and approach but also helps ensure team members understand and commit to the time and effort needed. The team develops products to present information obtained during data collection in a user-friendly format targeted at different audiences (e.g., youth, families). The team also needs to collaborate on a list of potential resources in the community (e.g., YMCA, independent living centers, adaptive recreational facilities). It is important to consider both the community's strengths and its possible shortcomings. These resources are important because they provide information to support secondary transition planning. The process should respond to questions such as:

- When does the team need the information?
- What methods will the team use to collect the information?
- What resources (people, copying, database creation and maintenance) does the team need to collect the information?
- Who is going to do what and by when?

Mapping and Problem Solving

Once the goals, priorities, and processes are in place, the team is ready to map its community's resources. This process distills information on locations of agencies or organizations, services provided, funding, and potential challenges or inadequacies. It also provides a way to gather information on other resources the team has not previously identified. Table 3.1 provides tips for collecting community-mapping information.

Table 3.1. Tips for Data Collection	
Use existing information resources	• Parents, individuals with disabilities • Chamber of Commerce • Phone book, Internet, newspaper • Previous inventories (e.g., independent living centers)
Think outside the box	• Web/e-mail surveys • Newspaper inserts • Community gatherings
Think ahead	• Remember the goal is to build a database • Use methods of data collection that can be easily entered

Some groups may want to use a city map and track information collected the old fashioned way, using bulletin boards and pushpins. Others may want to go more "high tech" and use mapping software (e.g., Google Maps, Google Earth) to track located resources. Community mapping goes beyond the creation of an actual map, however. It also involves collecting detailed information on the types of services provided by each identified resource. To compile these data—which is critical to the task of mapping the community's ability to support transitioning youth with disabilities—it is essential to visit each location. In addition to providing basic physical information on the location (e.g., is the site accessible to people with disabilities?), surveying and interviewing resource personnel will provide a clearer picture of how this particular agency or organization fits into the team's overall vision. Figure 3.2's Community Mapping Survey is a sample of the types of information that might be collected to inform community mapping. Collecting this type of comprehensive information will provide the team with the information it needs to align the resources within the community to the transition-specific areas of need (e.g., employment opportunities, postsecondary education supports) it has identified.

Figure 3.2. Community Mapping Survey

Date of visit: _____

Agency/organization: _____

Address: _____

Phone number: _____

Website: _____

Contact person (tel. # and e-mail address): _____

1. What services does the organization provide for youth with disabilities?

2. What services does the organization provide for adults with disabilities?

3. How are services funded? (What types of funding sources pay for services?)

4. What services does the organization plan to offer in the near future for youth with disabilities?

5. What critical elements does the organization lack regarding the support needs of students with disabilities?

6. What information can the organization share regarding other organizations in the community? (Other agencies or organizations serving the same population?)

7. Notes and observations: Is the site accessible to people with disabilities (doorways, restrooms, media/materials)? Does the agency seem to have the supplies, technology, and other supports it needs to effectively deliver services?

Consensus Building

After locating resources, the team will need to group them according to their areas of contribution (e.g., employment, independent living, recreation, postsecondary education). Figure 3.3 provides a template for team members to fill out after they have completed their assigned mapping activities. This report will allow the team members to share information with one another and evaluate the mapping process, determining what worked well and what did not.

Once a team has collected all the available information regarding supports for the target population, they can begin to prioritize needs through a consensus building process. *Consensus* is defined as "a decision in which everyone participates and with which everyone can live with and support" (Bowerman, Kohler, Coyle, Gothberg, & Shadrick, 2010, p. 29). Building consensus takes time. Prior to moving into action planning, the team should ensure key stakeholders have an adequate opportunity to discuss issues, work out any differences, and find areas of common ground.

Figure 3.3. Community Mapping Activity Report

Contact Name:_____

Organization:_____

How does the agency support or hinder youth transition planning and instruction?

Help	Hinder
_____	_____
_____	_____
_____	_____
_____	_____
_____	_____

Outline the services that the agency provides to support the transition needs of youth with disabilities as they prepare for postschool engagement.

1. _____

2. _____

3. _____

One beneficial strategy in helping teams attain their goals is *action planning*. Action planning is a process that results in a written action plan. The action plan should include the following components (a) the team's goals, (b) a list of actions or steps necessary to accomplish each goal, (c) the names of the team members responsible for carrying out the actions, and (d) timelines for accomplishing the actions (Kohler & Coyle, 2009; Test et al., 2006). The action plan should include additional information such as the resources the team will need to accomplish the team's goals, possible measures to assist in documenting the results of the team's actions, information regarding plans to meet and discuss progress, and procedures for sharing results. It is important to remember that action plans, as with IEPs, should be continuously monitored, evaluated, and adjusted. In order to see change you must continually revisit the data, prioritize needs based on data and context, develop goals, select strategies to support those goals, make decisions, plan actions, and evaluate results.

Research in Practice

After completing an initial process of pre-mapping, mapping, and reporting, Sophia Alverez' team was able to see all of the resources they had located and could establish whether or not the team had exhausted all the resources available to families and youth with disabilities in Caper. Specifically, the team determined they had exhausted all the resources for youth with intellectual disabilities in their community. Resources identified by the team to support (a) postsecondary education, included an 18-to-21-year-old program at Caper Community College and a community education program at the University of Caper; (b) postschool employment, included the Youth Transition Program and Caper Work Alternatives; and (c) independent living, included the Caper Transit System, Developmental Disability Services in Caper County, and Caper Independent Living Alliance. The team felt a need still existed to map the resources available for youth with learning disabilities (e.g., postsecondary education supports).

Summary

 Community mapping is an excellent method for telling a community story, making it an important piece of the transition planning process.

 Through community mapping, a team can highlight the rich array of community supports and services available for individuals with disabilities.

 After making a community map, a team will have assessed and identified resources within the community, enabling them to establish a relationship between the needs of youth with disabilities and the available services and supports in the community, including where services are lacking.

 Community mapping is a powerful way to identify and analyze existent or nonexistent patterns within the community, and it provides a visual method to communicate those patterns to a variety of stakeholders, facilitating change and promoting sustainability.

 Community mapping tells a story about programs and services within the local community and encourages decision making, problem solving, and consensus building to improve postschool outcomes for youth and adults with disabilities.

Chapter 4

Put It in Writing: Developing Collaborative Agreements

CEC-DCDT Collaboration Competencies for Transition Personnel addressed in this chapter...

Knowledge	Skills
• Strategies for collaborating with stakeholders to ensure and increase effective transition services, supports, and outcomes for youth with disabilities and their families.	• Promote active involvement of families, especially those from culturally and linguistically diverse backgrounds, throughout the transition decision-making and implementation processes. • Coordinate interagency agreements and partnerships to use and share data to achieve postsecondary outcomes. • Communicate with employers and other professionals to develop and monitor natural support networks. • Disseminate transition information and resources to stakeholders. • Participate in community-level transition teams. • Ensure compliance with federal and state policies affecting transition (e.g., Fair Labor Standards Act). • Implement student and family referrals to postsecondary and community services. • Communicate regularly with employers, businesses, and worksite personnel.

Collaboration among school personnel and community service agencies is imperative to ensure effective transition planning for youth with disabilities. Services are often administered by dozens of inflexible agencies and programs with diverse needs and objectives that have their own funding, guidelines, and requirements. Rules governing expenditure of funds and services provided vary as well (Steere, Rose, & Cavaiuolo, 2007). Without collaboration, it is difficult to align services and maximize benefits for youth with disabilities. Most important, unlike public education, there is no legal mandate for provision of services after a student leaves high school.

Establishing and maintaining a collaborative process early ensures that youth with disabilities receive the best possible assistance when transitioning from high school to postschool life (Harrison, n.d.; Office for Civil Rights, 2011).

This chapter will focus on three strategies schools can use to effectively implement the three models of collaboration discussed in Chapter 2: information exchange, responsibility transfer, and collaborative exchange. Tools such as the Summary of Performance (SOP), school- and district-level action plans, and interagency agreement support these strategies.

The Summary of Performance

The Summary of Performance (SOP) is one way to facilitate information exchange in the collaboration process. *Information exchange* involves the transfer of information (e.g., student records) among agencies with little or no coordinated planning or communication. The SOP can be a powerful document that can help youth with disabilities transition from school into postschool life; however, it is only a document. Without adequate communication among community service agencies and schools, the SOP could become nothing more than another piece of paperwork for school personnel and service providers to complete. The Individuals With Disabilities Education Act (IDEA, 2006) requires schools to provide an SOP for all students who have had an individualized education program, to support their transition from school into postschool life (see Figure 4.1). The SOP provides a summary of academic and functional performance and provides recommendations to assist in accomplishing postschool goals.

Figure 4.1. The Summary of Performance—in Simple Language	
Regulatory Language	**What It Means**
a child whose eligibility terminates due to graduation from secondary school with a regular diploma, or due to exceeding the age eligibility for FAPE under State law	A child with a disability who graduates or ages out
the public agency must provide a summary of the child's academic achievement and functional performance	The SOP must include a summary of academic achievement and a summary of functional performance
which shall include recommendations on how to assist the child in meeting the child's postsecondary goals.	The SOP must include recommendations to facilitate accomplishment of postschool goals

Note. Authority: 34 C.F.R. § 300.305(e)(3). Adapted with permission from *Review of the Literature Related to Summary Of Performance,* by S. Richter and V. L. Mazzotti (2009). Paper presented at the 15th International Division for Career Development and Transition Conference, Savannah, GA.

The SOP should be developed as part of the transition planning process and should involve input from a variety of stakeholders to ensure it meets the needs of youth with disabilities. The SOP facilitates communication with community service providers (Richter & Mazzotti, 2011). A comprehensive SOP will provide community service agencies, postsecondary education institutions (e.g., community colleges and universities), youth with disabilities, and families with a tool to minimize the gap that arises between what a student plans to do in postschool life and what the student actually does related to employment opportunities, education level, and independent living skills (Izzo & Kochhar-Bryant, 2006; Richter & Mazzotti, 2011). Special education teachers should ensure that the content of the SOP includes current information requested by the student, the community service providers, and the postsecondary education staff. Each postsecondary transition service provider has its own eligibility requirements (e.g., psychological assessment information within 3 years). To be proactive, schools should investigate the eligibility requirements of local postsecondary service providers during community mapping and include this information in the SOP.

Further, the SOP should be *student driven*, meaning that the student with a disability should be directly involved in its development. This includes providing opportunities for youth to contact community service providers and identify specific criteria for accessing services (Richter & Mazzotti, 2011). For example, a transition activity for a student may be to contact the disability services office at the local community college and request information about the services available and the specific evaluation criteria required to receive those services. There are a number of practical tips for developing the SOP that should be considered by special education teachers:

- Involve the student in developing the SOP during the last year of high school.
- Discuss development at a meeting where all stakeholders can attend.
- Remember that collaboration is critical.
- Include information essential for participation in postsecondary settings.
- Incorporate achievements, including up-to-date academic, personal, career, and employment levels of performance.
- Use results of current assessments.
- Include direct firsthand input from a variety of stakeholders.
- Use functional terms rather than jargon.
- Be familiar with college disability testing requirements (Grammer & Mazzotti, 2013).

Involving youth in the preparation of a well-developed SOP with input from a variety of stakeholders will benefit them as they transition into postschool life. Such involvement will help them (a) gain information about present levels of academic and functional performance, (b) set expectations for reasonable accommodations, and (c) self-identify and self-advocate in postschool employment and education settings (Grammer & Mazzotti, 2013; Mazzotti, Kelley, & Coco, 2015; Richter & Mazzotti, 2011). A well-developed SOP increases service coordination, improving access to services and resources as youth begin their adult experiences. It can improve access to technology in postschool settings and can prevent community service providers from having to start from scratch (Grammer & Mazzotti, 2013; Richter & Mazzotti, 2011). See Figure 4.2 for a sample SOP and Figure 4.3 for a checklist that can be used when developing the SOP.

Figure 4.2. Sample Summary of Performance

Demographic background information		
Student name:	Date of SOP:	Date of birth:
Student ID:	Year in school:	Graduation date:
Address:		
Home phone:	Cell phone:	Alternate phone:
E-mail address:		
Course of study:		

Transition assessment information (include information from informal and formal transition assessments here)
Formal assessments (include information from academic/psychological/adaptive behavior/vocational assessments):
Informal assessments (include information from dream sheets, parent/teacher/student interviews, ecological observations, task analysis, etc.):

Postschool goals	
Employment goal:	•
Education goal:	•
Independent living goal (if applicable):	•

Summary of academic performance (include student's present level of academic achievement and functional performance, accommodations, and modifications required to be successful in school)	
Summary of academic performance:	•
Summary of functional performance:	•
Accommodations:	• (attach *Review of Accommodations Used During Testing* form, or list accommodations if form is not attached)
Modifications:	•

Assistive technology (AT) (include assistive technology devices essential to the student's success in postsecondary settings; circle whether the device(s) is for academic and/or functional performance; include N/A if AT is not required)		
AT device:	•	academic functional
	•	academic functional
	•	academic functional

Recommendations (include recommendations to assist the student in meeting postsecondary goals, including suggestions for accommodations, assistive technology devices, assistive services, compensatory strategies, and support services to enhance success in postschool setting)
•

Student input (provide student comments and information regarding development of the SOP)
•

Completed SOP Checklist attached: Yes   No

Note. Developed by Valerie L. Mazzotti and Sharon M. Richter for the North Carolina Department of Public Instruction. Reprinted with permission.

Figure 4.3. Summary of Performance Checklist		
Questions	**Complete**	**Incomplete**
1. Does the SOP include all relevant demographic background information about the student (name, date of birth, contact information, projected graduation/departure date)?		
2. Are there formal and informal transition assessment reports that clearly document the student's disability and functional limitation attached?		
3. Is there an appropriate measurable postsecondary goal(s) in the area of employment from the student's most recent transition plan?		
4. Is there an appropriate measurable postsecondary goal(s) in the area of education from the student's most recent transition plan?		
5. If applicable, is there an appropriate measurable postsecondary goal(s) in the area of independent living from the student's most recent transition plan?		
6. Is there a summary of academic achievement (including present level of performance, accommodations, and modifications)?		
7. Is there a summary of functional performance (including present level of performance, accommodations, and modifications)?		
8. Are assistive technology devices essential to the student's success in postsecondary settings included (identify whether the device is for academic, cognitive, and/or functional performance)?		
9. Are the recommendations to assist the student in meeting postsecondary goals (include suggestions for accommodations, assistive technology devices, assistive services, compensatory strategies, and support services to enhance success in postsecondary setting)?		
10. Has the student provided input and information regarding development of the summary of performance?		
Does the SOP meet the requirements of IDEA? **Yes (each item is complete) No (1 or more items are incomplete)**		

Note. Developed by Valerie L. Mazzotti and Sharon M. Richter for the North Carolina Department of Public Instruction. Reprinted with permission.

Action Planning

Action planning is one way to facilitate responsibility transfer in the collaboration process. *Responsibility transfer* is the process of aligning services for students to ensure uninterrupted transition service delivery. When considering effective collaborative partnerships across school and community environments, it is necessary to ensure all stakeholders have a common mission and vision, including a strong commitment to support youth with disabilities through the transition process (Noonan, 2014; Noonan, Gaumer-Erickson, & Morningstar, 2013).

Action planning provides a framework to evaluate, improve, and expand transition programs for all youth with disabilities. A school-level team that collaborates on an action plan to provide integrated services towards a common goal will present a united front when developing relationships with community service providers.

There are a number of factors that must be considered when collaborating on behalf of youth with disabilities, including flexible scheduling, administrative support, relationship building, training faculty and staff, and disseminating information (Noonan, Morningstar, & Gaumer-Erickson, 2008). Although formal intra-agency agreements typically are unnecessary, it is important to develop action plans with school personnel to help guide day-to-day activities so the plan can support youth throughout the transition process.

Action planning is one strategy that can help teams attain their goals and is a process that results in a written plan. It should provide a framework to evaluate, improve, and expand transition programs for all youth with disabilities. Having an action plan in place can help facilitate relationships between families and school personnel, while minimizing barriers (Flexer, Baer, Luft, & Simmons, 2013). Further, a school-level team that collaborates on an action plan to provide integrated services toward a common goal will present a united front when developing relationships with community service providers. Through action planning, stakeholders can identify the effective characteristics of transition programs while also highlighting which students' transition needs are not being met (Noonan, 2014). Action planning should result in the development of a strategy for improving transition programs, practices, and services across the school and district.

Action planning is the "process that guides the day-to-day activities of an organization or project" (Shapiro, 2013, p. 4), and it typically encompasses five major action elements: identifying what needs to be achieved (i.e., the goal or goals), identifying steps that must be implemented to achieve the goal or goals, establishing a timeline for completion of each step, identifying who is responsible for making sure the step is completed, and identifying the resources required to complete each step (Kohler & Coyle, 2009; National Post-School Outcomes Center, 2013; Noonan, 2014; Shapiro, 2013; Test, Aspel, & Everson, 2006).

Prior to beginning action planning, however, it is essential for the school-level team to identify a framework for the work. Shapiro (2013) suggested six key components that should be in place prior to beginning the action planning process:

1. Establish a clear vision and understanding of the problem. What is the team's expectation for youth with disabilities to ensure a successful transition into adult life? What problems exist related to providing effective transition programs, practices, and services to youth with disabilities?

2. Establish a set of values to guide the work of the team. What outcomes does the team anticipate for youth with disabilities? What does the team hope to achieve?

3. Develop a clear mission statement. The mission statement should provide information about the goal of the team, how the team plans to accomplish the goal, and who will benefit from the plan (e.g., teachers, families, students).

4. Develop an overarching goal. The overarching goal should identify the specific problems that the team will address throughout the process (e.g., decrease the number of youth who are not engaged in the community after high school).

5. Define the purpose of the project. The purpose should include what the team plans to accomplish in the short- and midterm, including identifying specific objectives (e.g., increase the number youth participating in the transition planning process).

6. Identify key result areas. This should include expected results for specific objectives (e.g., increase professional development or implement evidence-based strategies).

Once this groundwork has been laid, it is time to develop an action plan to evaluate strengths, needs, and priorities for change in the school or district's secondary transition programs and practices. Any action that is identified as necessary must be specific, observable, and measurable. Further, the team must provide adequate detail to determine when the action step has been implemented.

In the first step of action planning, the team should develop a SMART goal (i.e., a goal that is specific, measurable, achievable, results focused, and time-bound; see Figure 4.4). A SMART goal should be started within 3 months, and the expectation is that it can be accomplished within 6 months to 1 year. The team should focus on what the school or district can accomplish over the course of a year to lay a strong foundation and prioritize a specific transition area (e.g., career awareness, parent involvement, self-advocacy or self-determination, community experiences, interagency collaboration, program of study).

Figure 4.4. The SMART Goals Model				
S	**M**	**A**	**R**	**T**
Specific	**Measurable**	**Achievable**	**Results focused**	**Time bound**
The activity must clearly state *what* is to be achieved, *by whom, where,* and *when.* It may also state *why* it is important that the activity is achieved.	The activity must clearly state how to evaluate whether the activity has been achieved. Think of the questions: *How much? How many? How often? How effective?* The goal is to measure change over time.	The activity must be achievable within the political climate, resources, and commitment of the SEA (e.g., provide additional development with current allotment of professional development days).	The activity must focus on outcomes (e.g., in-school or postschool outcomes of youth with disabilities) not the process.	The activity must clearly identify the timeline in which the activity is to be completed. This can include benchmarks and target date of completion (e.g., month/year).

Note. SEA = state education agency.

Research in Practice

Sophia Alverez worked with a school-level team at one high school in Caper to develop an action plan to increase the number of student-directed transition planning meetings. Sophia and the school team developed the plan to support a student-driven transition planning process to allow students to demonstrate self-awareness, goal setting, problem solving, and self-advocacy skills. The team identified specific steps to facilitate this process from professional development for teachers at Caper High School to implementation of student-led transition planning meetings. They specifically defined each step, including persons responsible, timelines, additional resources needed, and evaluation measures.

Once the school-level team has developed the SMART goal, it is time to develop the action plan (see sample, Figure 4.5). The action plan should include

- a notation of the focus area for improvement;
- a SMART goal, to be accomplished within the next 6 months to 1 year;
- next steps, which should include specific, observable, measurable steps that indicate what should be done to accomplish the goal;
- a list of responsible persons, including parties responsible for implementing each specific step;
- a due date, including a timeline for completing each step;
- a list of resources required for implementation of each step; and
- evaluation measures that will be used to evaluate progress towards the SMART goal.

Interagency Agreements

Developing and implementing interagency agreements (see Figure 4.6, end of this chapter) is one way to facilitate collaborative exchange. *Collaborative exchange* involves problem solving, sharing of information, and merging resources across agencies. In addition, effective interagency agreements include all key stakeholders who are committed to change. Interagency agreements (e.g., memorandums of understanding) "provide a clear, easy to follow road map for communities that will facilitate a smooth, comfortable transition" for families and youth with a disability from school district services to community services (Vocational Rehabilitation; Florida's Transition Project, n.d., p. 2). It is the responsibility of the community-level team to develop formal interagency agreements to help stakeholders collaborate between agencies at the state and local level (Butterworth, Foley, & Metzel, 2001).

Community-level teams (see Chapter 1) identify common goals, develop interagency agreements, and problem solve to facilitate collaboration among schools, families, and community service agencies. They typically create formal documents to be signed by administrators at each agency and can be developed at the state or local level (Butterworth et al., 2001). When developing an interagency agreement, team members must develop a shared vision for postschool outcomes. Also, the team must have an open communication system that tolerates disagreement and utilizes conflict resolution as a constructive means of moving forward. Table 4.1 delineates the process of developing and implementing interagency agreements.

Figure 4.5. Sample Action Plan

Area of Improvement: Utilize a student-driven IEP process to allow students to demonstrate self-awareness, goal setting, problem solving, and self-advocacy.

Team Goal: To increase the number of student-directed IEPs from 0 to 10 students by March 2015, the school will teach youth in two resource classrooms (i.e., 30 youth) how to lead their own IEP meetings using the Self-Advocacy Strategy (SAS).

Next Steps		Person(s) Responsible	Due Date
1	Provide professional development to two resource teachers on how to use the SAS.	District and school administrations Teachers	
2	Allow time for teachers to practice using the curriculum until they can implement with 100% fidelity.	District and school administrations Teachers	
3	Implement (SAS) in two resource rooms.	Teachers Students	
4	Assess student knowledge of strategy using SAS knowledge battery.	Teachers Students	
5	Allow students to practice directing their IEP meetings in a simulated environment.	Teachers Students Parents Counselor General education teacher School administrator	
6	Have students direct IEP meetings.	Students Teachers Parents Counselor Related service provider General education teacher School administrator Adult agency representative	

Needed Resources	Evaluation Measures
Professional development materials for implementing the SAS or expert trainer	• Indicator 13 • Student invitation to the IEP • Satisfactory student scores on SAS knowledge battery • IEP meeting notes • Student-developed IEP meeting materials

Notes:
- Meet every 2 weeks to discuss progress and possible changes needed in action plan.
- Time and location TBD.
- Results will be shared with local stakeholder group during last stakeholder group meeting of the school year.
- Parents will be informed of their child's progress during IEP meetings.

Note. IEP = individualized education program. The Self-Advocacy Strategy is a curriculum for teaching self-determination skills to youth with disabilities to support participation in the IEP process and includes a knowledge battery to assess self-advocacy skills. See http://www.edgeenterprisesinc.com/product_detail.php?product_id=87 for information about the curriculum.

Table 4.1. Developing and Implementing Interagency Agreements		
Phase 1: Research	• Identify existing relevant protocols that could be adapted for this purpose. • Identify key stakeholders (e.g., VR, developmental disabilities, other community partners). • Contact potential participants to seek preliminary support. • Organize initial meeting.	
Phase 2: Initial meeting(s)	• Clarify purpose of the interagency agreement (why it is needed, issues to be addressed, purpose of the agreement, and who is involved in implementation). • Elicit a shared commitment among stakeholders.	
Phase 3: Implementation	Step 1	Develop a process through which a group with cross-agency representation may develop a protocol (e.g., schedule weekly meetings to discuss the contents of the agreement).
	Step 2	Write a draft protocol document for circulation and feedback.
	Step 3	Finalize the protocol and distribute it to the appropriate authorities for signatures.
	Step 4	Develop a work group to oversee and support implementation of the agreement. Include staff training, staged implementation processes, a mechanism for early detection of issues or problems, and any additional resources or required supports.
	Step 5	Implement the agreement.
	Step 6	Establish a mechanism for regular monitoring and review of the agreement.
	Step 7	Revise the agreement as necessary.

The benefits to developing effective interagency agreements include (a) having a written record of specific guidelines and procedures, (b) clarifying roles and responsibilities for stakeholders, and (c) defining how each agency will work together (Florida's Transition Project, n.d.). Blalock (1996) proposed that interagency teams and activities are "critical for real change in transition programs and occur most meaningfully at the local level" (p. 149).

Components of Interagency Agreements

According to Butterworth et al. (2001), "good inter-agency agreements promote actions that directly or indirectly improve personal outcomes for those receiving services and promote systems change" (p. 1). The basic components of an interagency agreement include:

- statement of purpose,
- description of involved agencies,
- requirements affecting the agreement,
- definition of terms,
- working procedures and timelines,
- process for implementation of the agreement,
- process for monitoring and evaluating the agreement,
- process for conflict resolution, and
- signature and dates.

Summary

☑ Collaborative agreements are critical for facilitating real change in transition programs.

☑ There are several ways schools and community service providers can ensure youth with disabilities transition seamlessly into adult life.

☑ The SOP is a useful method of information exchange.

☑ Action planning expedites responsibility transfer, and interagency agreements facilitate collaborative exchange among inflexible and diverse agencies.

☑ On all fronts, early action will ensure youth with disabilities receive the best possible assistance when transitioning from high school to their postschool lives.

Figure 4.6. Interagency Agreement Template

INTERAGENCY AGREEMENT FOR TRANSITION SERVICES IN _____
PURPOSE

The purpose of this agreement is to facilitate the coordination of services to students with disabilities ages 14 and above (or younger if needed), within _____during the transition from school to employment and community living. For each individual to experience successful transition from school to postsecondary activities, an array of support and training opportunities are essential. A community-level transition team composed of parents, governmental agencies, community organizations, and private industry should collaborate to develop an appropriate service delivery system. To accomplish this task, the following services will be provided by each of the participating agencies.

This agreement is made and entered into between _____ and the local governmental and private agencies responsible for providing adult services to individuals with disabilities.

GENERAL RESPONSIBILITIES

  A. The agencies agree to support the development of regulations, policies, and practices for a community-level transition team.

  B. The agencies agree to exchange information regarding program goals and client needs when appropriate.

  C. The agencies agree to provide in-service training as needed.

  D. The agencies agree to provide representation at quarterly meetings for the purpose of evaluating and planning cooperative services.

  E. The agencies agree to provide representation on the school-level transition teams when necessary.

LOCAL EDUCATION AGENCIES AGREE TO:

  Provide the following services for students with disabilities based on need: (1) job placement, (2) job coaching (3) vocational assessment (4) vocational counseling (5) modified curriculum (6) service coordination (7) job follow-up until exit from school (8) follow-up annually after graduation or exit from school for a period of 3 years for the purpose of program evaluation.

Figure 4.6. Interagency Agreement Template (cont'd)

THE COMMUNITY AGENCIES

Mental Health, Developmental Disabilities and Substance Abuse Services Agree to:

- Support transition services to young adults with developmental disabilities.
- Provide the following: routine consultation with other agencies, referrals to residential services, vocational follow-up, and postgraduation counseling.
- Provide certification of students for determining adult services eligibility.
- Attend scheduled conferences for transitioning students when appropriate before they exit the school program.
- Provide case management services for eligible students.

Community College Agrees to:

- Provide services to students who have been admitted to the community college system.
- Support and assist youth with disabilities in job training and assessment through enrollment in the curriculum program.
- Provide job placement services, career exploration and counseling opportunities, job-seeking skills training, and financial aid to eligible students.
- Help eligible students access compensatory education and adult basic education classes.
- Attend scheduled conferences for transitioning students when appropriate before they exit the school program.

The Community Rehabilitation Agency Agrees to:

- Support transitional services to identified young adults who are developmentally disabled.
- Coordinate and assist with referral of students to the community rehabilitation agency.
- Provide the following services to eligible clients: vocational evaluation, vocational skills training, job placement, job coaching, case coordination, long-term follow-up, and short-term follow-up.
- Attend scheduled conferences for transitioning students when appropriate before they exit the school program.

Figure 4.6. Interagency Agreement Template (cont'd)

Department of Social Services Agrees to:

- Support transition services of young adults with developmental disabilities.
- Provide routine consultation with other agencies making referrals for residential and transportation services.
- Assist in the coordination of Work First programs and transition services.
- Assist with guardianship issues.
- Attend scheduled conferences for transitioning students when appropriate before they exit school.

Employment Security Commission (Job-Link Center) Agrees to:

- Provide transition services to any U.S. citizen or individual authorized to work by the Immigration and Naturalization Service, who is of legal age.
- Provide services by distributing labor market and career information along with appropriate and suitable job placement assistance to eligible clients.
- Attend scheduled conferences for transitioning students when appropriate before they exit the school program.

Workforce Investment Act Program Agrees to:

- Support transition services of economically disadvantaged youth.
- Provide services through career planning, career assessment, job training, apprenticeships, job placement, support for educational services, and support services to eligible and suitable clients.
- Attend scheduled conferences for transitioning students when appropriate before they exit school.

The Recreation Department Agrees to:

- Support transition services of individuals with disabilities.
- Provide services through various recreational opportunities and facilities.
- Attend scheduled conferences for transitioning students when appropriate before they exit the school program.

Figure 4.6. Interagency Agreement Template (cont'd)

The Local Transportation Authority Agrees to:

- Provide social service agency transportation under a single provider concept to clients of public and private nonprofit agencies.
- Provide transportation to the general public on a private contract basis.
- Support transition services to individuals with disabilities through consultation services to teachers, students, and parents.
- Attend scheduled conferences for transitioning students when appropriate before they exit school.

Vocational Rehabilitation Agrees to:

- Support transition services of individuals with disabilities that will result in an employment outcome.
- Coordinate referrals of vocational rehabilitation clients.
- Sponsor in-school adjustment training and job coaching services.
- Provide vocational evaluations, counseling, training, and transportation assistance to eligible individuals based on need.
- Provide follow-up services for employed students who have exited the school system.
- Provide all services indicated in the cooperative school system vocational rehabilitation agreement.
- Attend scheduled conferences of students in transition when appropriate before they exit the school program.

Social Security Administration Agrees to:

- Assist students and their families in determining eligibility for benefits.
- Assist students and their families in accessing work incentives.
- Provide consultation to school personnel regarding social security benefits and related issues.
- Attend scheduled conferences for transitioning students when appropriate before they exit the school program.

This agreement will be renegotiated on an annual basis. This agreement is being entered into on _____.

Note: Signatures of Representatives of Participating Agencies should be attached.

Note. Adapted with permission from Shelby City Schools, TASSEL, 1997.

Conclusion

Revisiting Collaborative Strategies for Effective Transition

As schools and community service providers move forward in the collaboration process, it is imperative that they develop community-, school-, and individual-level teams to ensure youth with disabilities transition successfully into postschool life. Collaboration is "a clear, purposeful, and carefully designed process that promotes cross-agency, cross-program, and cross-disciplinary collaborative efforts leading to tangible transition outcomes for youth" (Rowe et al., 2015, p. 122). When creating teams, it is important to:

- Develop wide-reaching state interagency teams that include disability-related and nondisability-related agencies (e.g., developmental disabilities, vocational rehabilitation, labor, social security) with a common interest in transition service delivery.
- Develop and implement formal and informal agreements between agencies responsible for the delivery of transition services.
- Develop an agreed upon vision and mission of transition services and programs.
- Develop an organizational structure that includes a process for identifying membership (e.g., criteria for membership), terms of services, procedures for replacing members, orientation for new members, and web-based and print membership directories.
- Coordinate the development of policies and procedures for service delivery and resource sharing by school and community agencies.
- Implement a statewide plan that (a) addresses gaps, (b) includes strategies for blending and braiding funding of other resources, (c) streamlines the transition process, and (d) eradicates duplication of service delivery.
- Conduct asset and resource mapping to identify all community agencies that support youth with disabilities in the area as well as gaps in service delivery.
- Clearly define the roles and responsibilities of each organization as part of the interagency agreement.
- Schedule regular times to plan, develop, and measure the progress and effectiveness of a shared transition service delivery system at all levels (i.e., individual student, school, local, regional, state, and nation).
- Develop procedures for shared problem solving to address needs of students with disabilities and the barriers they may face during transition.
- Develop procedures for school staff to systematically include students, families, community members, and agencies at different levels of the transition process (e.g., when to invite to IEP meetings, when to refer families to meet with an agency, when to provide an information sheet to the family).

- Establish multiple methods of communication across agencies.
- Provide cross-discipline professional development opportunities for all members of the interagency council to ensure members are knowledgeable about services and eligibility criteria (Rowe et al., 2015, p. 122).

Collaborative teams that are implemented with these elements in place can have wide reaching effects on the transition process. Collaborative teams can (a) promote effective and efficient coordination of services and resources, (b) advocate for new services and resources, (c) facilitate removal of barriers to policy and practice, and (d) encourage continued evaluation to ensure programs are implemented effectively and are sustained to improve outcomes for youth with disabilities (Test, Aspel, & Everson, 2006). Finally, it is important to remember effective collaboration increases the likelihood of youth with disabilities positively engaging in their communities after high school (e.g., working, learning, and living).

References

Aspel, N., Bettis, G., Quinn, P., Test, D. W., & Wood, W. M. (1999). A collaborative process for planning transition services for all students with disabilities. *Career Development for Exceptional Individuals, 22,* 21–41. doi: http://dx.doi.org/10.1177/088572889902200103

Benz, M. R., Lindstrom, L. E., & Halpern, A. S. (1995). Mobilizing local communities to improve transition services. *Career Development for Exceptional Individuals, 18,* 21–32. doi: http://dx.doi.org/10.1177/088572889501800103

Benz, M. R., Lindstrom, L. E., & Latta, T. (1999). Improving collaboration between schools and vocational rehabilitation: The youth transition program model. *Journal of Vocational Rehabilitation, 13,* 55–63.

Blalock, G. (1996). Community transition teams as the foundation for transition services for youth with learning disabilities. *Journal of Learning Disabilities, 29,* 145–159. doi: http://dx.doi.org/10.1177/002221949602900204

Blalock, G., Kocchar-Bryant, C. A., Test, D. W., Kohler, P., White, W., Lehman, J., & Patton, J. (2003). The need for comprehensive personnel preparation in transition and career development: A position statement of the Division on Career Development and Transition. *Career Development for Exceptional Individuals, 26,* 207–226. doi: 10.1177/088572880302600207

Bowerman, R. L., Kohler, P. D., Coyle, J. L., Gothberg, J., & Shadrick, I. D. (2010). *Facilitator preparation manual.* Kalamazoo, MI: Western Michigan University, National Secondary Transition Technical Assistance Center.

Bullis, M., Davis, C., Bull, B., & Johnson, B. (1995). Transition achievement among young adults with deafness: What variables relate to success? *Rehabilitation Counseling Bulletin, 39,* 103–150.

Butterworth, J., Foley, S., & Metzel, D. (2001, December). *Institute brief: Developing interagency agreements: Four questions to consider* (Paper No. 14). Boston, MA: Institute for Community Inclusion.

Campbell-Whatley, G. D., & Lyons, J. E. (2013). *Leadership practices for special and general educators.* Boston, MA: Pearson.

Collet-Klingenberg, L. (1998). The reality of best practices in transition: A case study. *Exceptional Children, 65,* 67–78.

Condon, E., & Callahan, M. (2008). Individualized career planning for students with significant support needs utilizing the discovery and vocational profile process, cross-agency collaborative funding and social security work incentives. *Journal of Vocational Rehabilitation, 28,* 85–96.

Council for Exceptional Children. (2013, October). *Specialty set: CEC advanced special education transition specialist.* Retrieved from http://www.dcdt.org/cec-transition-standards/

Crane, K., & Mooney, M. (2005). *Community resource mapping.* Retrieved from the National Center on Secondary Education and Transition website: http://www.ncset.org/publications/essentialtools/mapping/

Devlieger, P., & Trach, J. (1999). Meditation as a transition process: The impact on postschool employment outcomes. *Exceptional Children, 65,* 507–523.

Everson, J. M., & Guillory, J. D. (2002). *Interagency teaming: Strategies for facilitating teams from forming through performing.* Baton Rouge, LA: University Center of Excellence in Developmental Disabilities Education, Research, and Services, Louisiana State University Health Sciences Center.

Fabian, E. S., Luecking, R. G., & Tilson, G. P. (1994). *A working relationship: The job-development specialist's guide to successful partnerships with businesses.* Baltimore, MD: Brookes.

Fixsen, D. L., Blasé, K. A., Duda, M. A., Naoom, S. F., & VanDyke, M. (2009, May). *Sustaining interventions and improving post-school outcomes.* Paper presented at the annual Secondary Transition State Planning Institute, Charlotte, NC.

Flexer, R. W., Baer, R. M., Luft, P., & Simmons, T. J. (2013). *Transition planning for secondary students with disabilities* (4th ed.). Baltimore, MD: Pearson Education.

Florida's Transition Project. (n.d.). *Developing interagency agreements: The road map for transition.* Author. Retrieved from http://www.floridatransitionproject.ucf.edu/resources/TheRoadMapforTransition.pdf

Gowdy, E. L., Carlson, L. S., & Rapp, C. A. (2003). Practices differentiating high-performing from low-performing supported employment programs. *Psychiatric Rehabilitation Journal, 26,* 232–239. doi: http://dx.doi.org/10.2975/26.2003.232.239

Grammer, B., & Mazzotti, V. L. (2013, April). *Meeting the secondary transition requirements of IDEA.* Paper presented at the North Carolina Career Development and Transition 2013 Annual Conference, Greensboro, NC.

Hands, C. M. (2010). Why collaborate? The differing reasons for secondary school educators' establishment of school-community partnerships. *School Effectiveness and School Improvement, 21,* 189–207. doi: 10.1080/09243450903553993

Harrison, B. (n.d.). *Effective strategies for interagency collaboration.* Retrieved from http://www.transitiononestop.org/HSCInteragencyCollaboration.ashx

Hein, V., Smerdon, B., & Sambolt, M. (2013, November). *Predictors of postsecondary success.* Retrieved from http://www.ccrscenter.org/products-resources/predictors-postsecondary-success

Hentz, S. M., & Jones, P. M. (2011). *Collaborate smart: Practical strategies and tools for educators.* Arlington, VA: Council for Exceptional Children.

Hughes, C., & Carter, E. W. (2012). *The new transition handbook: Strategies high school teachers use that work.* Baltimore, MD: Paul H. Brookes.

Individuals With Disabilities Education Act, 20 U.S.C. § 1400 *et seq.* (2006 & Supp. 2011).

Individuals With Disabilities Education Act Regulations, 34 C.F.R. § 300 (2012).

Izzo, M., & Kochhar-Bryant, C. (2006). Implementing the SOP for effective transition: Two case studies. *Career Development for Exceptional Individuals, 29,* 100–107. doi: http://dx.doi.org/10.1177/08857288060290020101

Johnson, D. R., Bruininks, R. H., & Thurlow, M. L. (1987). Meeting the challenge of transition service planning through improved interagency cooperation. *Exceptional Children, 53,* 522–530.

Katsiyannis, A., Zhang, D., Woodruf, N., & Dixon, A. (2005). Transition supports to students with mental retardation: An examination of data from the National Longitudinal Transition Study 2. *Education and Training in Developmental Disabilities, 40,* 109–116.

Kohler, P. D., & Coyle, J. L. (2009). *Transition institute toolkit.* Kalamazoo, MI: The Western Michigan University National Secondary Transition Technical Assistance Center.

Kohler, P. D., & Field, S. (2003). Transition-focused education: Foundation for the future. *The Journal of Special Education, 37,* 174–183. doi: http://dx.doi.org/10.1177/00224 669030370030701

Mazzotti, V. L. (2009, October) *Interagency collaboration annotated bibliography.* Charlotte, NC: National Secondary Transition Technical Assistance Center.

Mazzotti, V. L., Kelley, K. R., & Coco, C. (2015). Effects of Self-Directed Summary of Performance on postsecondary students' participation in Person-Centered Planning. *The Journal of Special Education, 48,* 243-255. doi:10.1177/0022466913483575

Morningstar, M., Gaumer-Erickson, A., & Noonan, P. (2009, October). *Transition and multitiered systems of support: How does it all fit together?* Paper presented at the Division of Career Development and Transition Conference, Savanna, GA.

Morningstar, M. E., Bassett, D. S., Kochhar-Bryant, C., Cashman, J., & Wehmeyer, M. L., (2012). Aligning transition services with secondary education reform: A position statement of the Division of Career Development and Transition. *Career Development and Transition for Exceptional Individuals, 35,* 132–143. doi: 10.1177/2165143412454915

Morningstar, M. E., & Clark, G. M. (2003). The status of personnel preparation for transition education and services: What is the critical content? How can it be offered? *Career Development for Exceptional Individuals, 26,* 227–237. doi: http://dx.doi. org/10.1177/088572880302600208

National High School Center, National Center on Response to Intervention, & Center on Instruction. (2010). *Tiered interventions in high school: Using preliminary "lessons learned" to guide ongoing discussion.* Washington, DC: American Institutes for Research. Retrieved from http://www.ccrscenter.org/products-resources/resource-database/tiered-interventions-high-schools-using-preliminary-%E2%80%9Clessons

National Post-School Outcomes Center. (2013). *State toolkit for examining post-school success: Facilitator's guide.* Eugene: University of Oregon.

Newman, L., Wagner, M., Knokey, A.-M., Marder, C., Nagle, K., Shaver, D., ... Schwarting, M.. (2011, September). *The post-high school outcomes of young adults with disabilities up to 8 years after high school: A report from the National Longitudinal Transition Study-2 (NLTS2;* NCSER 2011–3005). Menlo Park, CA: SRI International. Retrieved from www.nlts2.org/reports/

Noonan, P. (2014). *Transition teaming: 26 strategies for interagency collaboration.* Arlington, VA: Council for Exceptional Children.

Noonan, P. M., Gaumer-Erickson, A., & Morningstar, M. E. (2013). Effects of community transition teams on interagency collaboration for school and adult agency staff. *Career Development and Transition for Exceptional Individuals, 36,* 96–104. doi: http://dx.doi.org/10.1177/2165143412451119

Noonan, P. M., Morningstar, M. E., & Clark, G. M. (2005). *Assessment and transition: The big picture.* The University of Kansas Transition Coalition, Department of Special Education. Retrieved from http://www.transitioncoalition.org/cgiwrap/tcacs/new/resources/presentations/index.php

Noonan, P. M., Morningstar, M. E., & Gaumer-Erickson, A. (2008). Improving interagency collaboration: Effective strategies used by high performing local districts and communities. *Career Development for Exceptional Individuals, 31,* 132–143. doi: http://dx.doi.org/10.1177/0885728808327149

Office for Civil Rights. (2011). *Transition of students with disabilities to postsecondary education: A guide for high school educators.* Washington, DC: U.S. Department of Education.

Parent, W., & Wehman, P. (2011). Writing the transition individualized education program. In P. Wehman, *Essentials of Transition Planning.* (pp. 95-110). Baltimore, MD: Brookes.

Peterson, R. L., & Roessler, R. T. (1997). Improving collaborative school-agency transition planning: A statewide DBMS approach. *Journal of Vocational Rehabilitation, 8,* 259–267. doi: http://dx.doi.org/10.1016/S1052-2263(97)00009-3

Povenmire-Kirk, T., Crump, K., Dieglemann, K., & Schnorr, C. (2013, May). *CIRCLES interagency collaboration in transition: An efficient, effective service delivery model.* Paper presented at the Seventh Annual Capacity Building Institute, Charlotte, NC.

Repetto, J. B., Webb, K. W., Garvan, C. W., & Washington, T. (2002). Connecting student outcomes with transition practices in Florida. *Career Development for Exceptional Individuals, 25,* 123–139. doi: http://dx.doi.org/10.1177/088572880202500203

Richter, S. M., & Mazzotti, V. L. (2009, October). *Review of the literature related to summary of performance.* Paper presented at the 15th International Division for Career Development and Transition Conference, Savannah, GA.

Richter, S. M., & Mazzotti, V. L. (2011, December). A comprehensive review of the literature on summary of performance. *Career Development for Exceptional Individuals, 34*(3), 176–186. doi: 10.1177/0885728811399089

Rowe, D. A., Alverson, C. Y., Unruh, D., Fowler, C., Kellems, R., & Test, D. W. (2015). A Delphi study to operationalize evidence-based predictors in secondary transition. *Career Development and Transition for Exceptional Individuals, 38,* 113-126. doi: 10.1177/2165143414526429

Rutgers Safe and Drug Free Schools Community Project. (2009). *Strategies for effective collaboration with parents, schools, and community members.* Retrieved from http://sdfsc.rutgers.edu/file/Workshop%20Handouts/CH%20Effective%20Collaboration%2009.pdf

Rutkowski, S., Daston, M., VanKuiken, D., & Riehle, E. (2006). Project SEARCH: A demand-side model of high school transition. *Journal of Vocational Rehabilitation, 25,* 85–96.

Shapiro, J. (2013). *Action planning toolkit.* Retrieved from http://www.civicus.org/new/media/Action%20Planning.pdf

Steere, D. E., Rose, E., & Cavaiuolo, D. (2007). *Growing up: Transition to adult life for students with disabilities.* Boston, MA: Pearson Education.

Stodden, R. A., Brown, S. E., Galloway, L. M., Mrazek, S., & Noy, L. (2004). *Essential tools: Interagency transition team development and facilitation.* Minneapolis, MN: University of Minnesota Institute on Community Integration, National Center on Secondary Education and Transition.

Storms, J., O'Leary, E., & Williams, J. (2000). *The Individuals with Disabilities Education Act of 1997 transition requirements: A guide for states, districts, schools, universities and families.* Minneapolis, MN: University of Minnesota National Center on Secondary Education and Transition, Institute on Community Integration.

Test, D. W., Aspel, N. P., & Everson, J. M. (2006). *Transition methods for youth with disabilities.* Upper Saddle River, NJ: Pearson Merrill Prentice Hall.

Test, D. W., Mazzotti, V. L., Mustian, A. L., Fowler, C. H., Kortering, L. J., & Kohler, P. H. (2009). Evidence-based secondary transition predictors for improving post-school outcomes for students with disabilities. *Career Development for Exceptional Individuals, 32,* 160–181. doi: http://dx.doi.org/10.1177/0885728809346960

Test, D. W., Morningstar, M. M., Lombardi, A., & Fowler, C. (2013, November). *Data-based decision making: Creating a secondary focused multi-tiered system of support.* Paper presented at the Midyear Check and Connect: Williamsburg, VA.

Thomas, S. B., & Dykes, F. (2011). Promoting successful transitions: What can we learn from RTI to enhance outcomes for all students. *Preventing School Failure, 55*(1), 1–9. doi: 10.1080/10459880903217978

Wandry, D. L., & Pleet, A. M. (Eds.). (2009). *Engaging and empowering families in secondary transition: A practitioner's guide.* Arlington, VA: Council for Exceptional Children.

Wehman, P., Moon, M. S., Everson, J. M., Wood, W., & Barcus, J. M. (1988). *Transition from school to work: More challenges for youth with severe disabilities.* Baltimore, MD: Brookes.

Wood, C. L., Kelley, K. R., Test, D. W., & Fowler, C. H. (2010). Comparing audio-supported text and explicit instruction on students' knowledge of accommodations, rights, and responsibilities. *Career Development for Exceptional Individuals, 33,* 115–124. doi: 10.1177/0885728810361618